Teaching for Kids with Dyslexia

A Wealth of Practical Ideas and Teaching Strategies That Can Help Children with Dyslexia (and Other Reading Disabilities) Become Successful Readers!

by
Sherrill B. Flora

illustrated by
Timothy M. Irwin

Publisher
Key Education Publishing Company, LLC
Minneapolis, Minnesota 55431

www. keyeducationpublishing.com

CONGRATULATIONS ON YOUR PURCHASE OF A KEY EDUCATION PRODUCT!

The editors at Key Education are former teachers who bring experience, enthusiasm, and quality to each and every product. Thousands of teachers have looked to the staff at Key Education for new and innovative resources to make their work more enjoyable and rewarding. Key Education is committed to developing and publishing educational materials that will assist teachers in building a strong and developmentally appropriate curriculum for young children.

PLAN FOR GREAT TEACHING EXPERIENCES WHEN YOU USE
EDUCATIONAL MATERIALS FROM KEY EDUCATION PUBLISHING COMPANY, LLC

Resources for Parents and Teachers

The Council for Exceptional Children
Division for Learning Disabilities

1110 N. Glebe Rd., Suite 300 • Arlington, VA 22201-5704
Phone: 1-888-CEC-SPED • *URL:* www.teachingld.org
The Division for Learning Disabilities (DLD) is a special interest group of the Council for Exceptional Children (CEC), an international professional organization dedicated to improving educational outcomes for individuals with exceptionalities and students with disabilities. DLD works on behalf of students with learning disabilities and the professionals who serve them.

The International Dyslexia Association

40 York Road, 4th Floor
Baltimore, MD 21204
Phone: 1-410-296-0232 • *URL:* www.interdys.org
The International Dyslexia Association (IDA) is a scientific and educational organization dedicated to the study and treatment of dyslexia. IDA focuses its resources in four major areas: information and referral services, research, advocacy, and direct services to professionals in the field of learning disabilities.

Learning Disabilities Association of America

4156 Library Road • Pittsburgh, PA 15234-1349
Phone: 1-412-341-1515 • *URL:* www.ldaamerica.org
The Learning Disabilities Association of America (LDA) is an organization founded by parents of children with learning disabilities. The LDA works to provide education, encourage research into learning disabilities, create a climate of public awareness, and provide advocacy information and training.

LD OnLine

WETA Public Television
2775 S. Quincy Street • Arlington, VA 22206
URL: www.ldonline.org
LD OnLine is an educational service of public television station WETA in association with the National Joint Committee on Learning Disabilities. It features hundreds of articles on learning and reading disabilities, monthly columns by experts, a free question-and-answer service, and a directory of professionals and services.

National Center for Learning Disabilities

381 Park Avenue S., Suite 1401 • New York, NY 10016
Phone: 1-888-575-7373 • *URL:* www.ncld.org
The National Center for Learning Disabilities (NCLD) is an organization devoted to working with individuals with LD, their families, educators, and researchers. NCLD provides essential information, promotes research and programs to foster effective learning, and advocates for policies to protect and strengthen educational rights and opportunities.

Credits
Author: Sherrill B. Flora
Creative Director: Annette Hollister-Papp
Cover Design: Annette Hollister-Papp
Illustrator: Timothy M. Irwin
Editors: Karen Seberg and Claude Chalk
Production: Key Education Staff

Key Education welcomes manuscripts and product ideas from teachers.
For a copy of our submission guidelines, please send a self-addressed, stamped envelope to:
Key Education Publishing Company, LLC
Acquisitions Department
9601 Newton Avenue South • Minneapolis, Minnesota 55431

References

Capirci, O., Cattani, A., Rossinni P., Volterra, V. 1998. "Teaching sign language to hearing children as a possible factor in cognitive enhancement." *Journal of Deaf Studies and Deaf Education* 3 (Spring): 135–142.

Chall, Dr. Jeanne S. 1983. *Stages of Reading Development*. New York: McGraw Hill.

Daniels, M. 1994. "The effects of sign language on hearing children's language development." *Sign Language Studies* 78:25–30.

International Reading Association, Division of Research and Policy. 2002. *Summary of the National Reading Panel Report: Teaching Children to Read.* http://www.reading.org/downloads/resources/nrp_summary.pdf/.

National Institute for Literacy—The Partnership for Reading. "Glossary of Terms." http://www.nifl.gov/partnershipforreading/glossary/glossary.html/.

National Institutes of Health. April, 2000. *Report of the National Reading Panel: Teaching Children to Read.* "Findings and Determinations of the National Reading Panel by Topic Areas." http://www.nichd.nih.gov/publications/nrp/findings.cfm/.

Introduction

Dyslexia is the most common cause of reading, writing, and spelling difficulties. *Teaching Tips for Kids with Dyslexia* was written for anyone interested in learning more about dyslexia and acquiring a variety of strategies that can help these children become successful students!

Research has shown that possibly as many as 43 million Americans, from all economic and ethnic backgrounds, have dyslexia. In addition, research indicates that a predisposition to dyslexia can run in families. A family history of dyslexia could mean that as many as one-quarter to one-half of the children born to a parent with dyslexia will also have dyslexia, and that if one child in a family has dyslexia, almost half of that child's siblings will also have dyslexia.

Here is the good news! Children with dyslexia can learn to read; are often very bright and verbal; and are frequently highly creative with superior reasoning abilities. The earlier children with dyslexia are identified, the easier it is to remediate their potential problems. When a diagnosis occurs after third grade, a child's dyslexia is much more difficult to treat. Consequently, the observations of parents and preschool, kindergarten, and first-grade teachers are crucial. If you suspect that a child may have a language or learning delay, seek an evaluation. Do not wait until that child is failing and falling significantly behind the child's peers.

Teaching Tips for Kids with Dyslexia is filled with information, suggestions, and teaching strategies that will help parents and teachers build a solid foundation for developing early reading skills in young children with dyslexia.

Contents

Chapter One
Understanding Dyslexia

What Is Dyslexia?

The word *dyslexia* comes from the Greek word *dys* (meaning "poor" or "difficult") and the word *lexis* (meaning "word"). The literal translation is "poor words" or "difficult words."

The **National Institute of Child Health and Human Development (NICHD)**, 2002, defines dyslexia as "a specific learning disability that is neurological in origin. It is characterized by difficulties with accurate and/or fluent word recognition and by poor spelling and decoding abilities. These difficulties typically result from a deficit in the phonological component of language that is often unexpected in relation to other cognitive abilities and the provision of effective classroom instruction. Secondary consequences may include problems in reading comprehension and reduced reading experience that can impede growth of vocabulary and background knowledge."

According to the **International Dyslexia Association's Committee of Members** in November, 1994, "Dyslexia is a neurologically-based, often familial, disorder which interferes with the acquisition and processing of language. Varying in degrees of severity, it is manifested by difficulties in receptive and expressive language, including phonological processing, in reading, writing, spelling, handwriting, and sometimes in arithmetic. Dyslexia is not a result of lack of motivation, sensory impairment, inadequate instructional or environmental opportunities, or other limiting conditions, but may occur together with these conditions. Although dyslexia is life-long, individuals with dyslexia frequently respond successfully to timely and appropriate intervention."

According to the **International Dyslexia Association's Research Committee** in November, 1994, "Dyslexia is one of several distinct learning disabilities. It is a specific language-based disorder of constitutional origin characterized by difficulties in single word decoding, usually reflecting insufficient phonological processing abilities. These difficulties in single word decoding are often unexpected in relation to age and other cognitive and academic abilities; they are not the result of generalized developmental disability or sensory impairment. Dyslexia is manifested by variable difficulty with different forms of language, often including, in addition to problems reading, a conspicuous problem with acquiring proficiency in writing and spelling."

And finally, according to the **U.S. Department of Health and Human Services**, "Developmental dyslexia is a specific learning disability characterized by difficulty in learning to read. Some dyslexics also may have difficulty learning to write, to spell, and sometimes, to speak or to work with numbers. We do not know for sure what causes dyslexia, but we do know that it affects children who are physically and emotionally healthy, academically capable, and who come from good home environments. In fact, many dyslexics have the advantages of excellent schools, high mental ability, and parents who are well-educated and value learning."

In other words:

❑ Dyslexia is a language-based disorder that can make learning—to read, write, and spell, and sometimes to comprehend mathematics—difficult.

❑ People with dyslexia are smart and can learn to read with proper instruction.

❑ People with dyslexia are not lazy but are faced with the challenge of a unique learning style.

Prevalence—Who Has Dyslexia?

The following statistics may be surprising, but they have also led to new research and the development of successful teaching strategies:

❏ The National Institutes of Health estimate that approximately 15 percent of the U.S. population is affected by learning disabilities.

❏ Of the students with learning disabilities receiving special education services, 80 to 85 percent have deficits in language and reading.

❏ According to the U.S. Department of Education statistics, approximately 4.5 percent of American students—slightly more than 2.5 million children—receive special educational services for a reading disorder.

❏ Researchers have concluded that possibly as many as 43 million Americans, from all economic and ethnic backgrounds, have dyslexia.

❏ Dyslexia is the most common cause of reading, writing, and spelling difficulties.

❏ Students with untreated dyslexia are more likely to drop out of high school and become unemployed, underemployed, or incarcerated.

❏ And . . . anyone, from any place and any ethnic group, can have dyslexia, including some of the most famous, successful, and influential people throughout history.

Dyslexia and Current Brain Research

Beginning in the early 1990s, with the improved technology of functional brain imaging, researchers and scientists funded by the National Health Institute were able to look at images of the brain and view how the brain worked while people were engaged in reading. This allowed researchers to actually see how the brain translates print (letters) into language (spoken sounds). This research also provided clear evidence that there are distinct differences in how the brain functions between people with dyslexia and people who do not have dyslexia.

To provide a better understanding, the following section looks at how **oral language** is acquired and then what is required for children to learn how to read **written language**.

Oral Language: To communicate effectively, we use a language system comprised of four levels.

❏ The lowest level of the language system is **phonology**—the sound elements of language. The smallest individual sound elements are called phonemes. There are 44 individual phonemes in the English language, which can be combined into literally endless combinations of words. For example, when the individual phonemes /d/, /o/, and /g/ are retrieved from memory and blended together, they become the spoken word *dog*. (See pages 26 and 27 for the entire list of phonemes.)

❏ The next level is **semantics**—vocabulary and word meaning.

❏ The third level is **syntax**—the grammatical structure of language.

❏ And, the final level is **discourse**—how sentences are connected to create meaningful communication.

Although our language system may sound complicated, people do not have to be taught how to speak. The human brain seems to be naturally wired for language. To learn language, human infants simply need to be around other humans who speak. People automatically learn the smallest parts of speech (phonemes) and are able to combine phonemes into words.

Written Language: Unfortunately, human brains do not seem to be naturally wired to read. Children do not simply acquire the ability to read from being around people who can read. Reading has to be taught. Children must develop an understanding of and the ability to look at printed letters and convert those letters into a phonetic or linguistic code. This knowledge is called the *alphabetic principle*. Unless a child can apply the alphabetic principle, letters are simply meaningless squiggles on paper.

Approximately 70 to 80 percent of American children learn to read without much trouble. They become aware that spoken words are broken down into smaller units of sound (phonemic awareness) and that those sounds are attached to written letters—the letters begin to have meaning. All children must go through the same stages of reading whether they have dyslexia or not. (See Chall's Stages of Reading Development, page 12.)

The remaining 20 to 30 percent of children have a great deal of difficulty making this connection. They struggle to acquire phonemic awareness, which leads to an inability to link letters to sounds, thus creating many challenges in learning how to read.

Conclusions and Implications of Brain Research

Doctors Sally Shaywitz and her husband, Bennett Shaywitz (Yale University School of Medicine), first used brain imaging to determine that the ability to learn to read is located in the left hemisphere of the brain and that three parts of the brain in this hemisphere work together to help people learn to read. One part recognizes phonemes, another part connects the phonemes to the letters that represent them, and the third part serves as long-term memory storage. In other words, once a word is learned, the brain will store it and automatically recognize it. People who struggle to read were found to use the first two areas of the brain but then had difficulty accessing the long-term memory area, consequently making the quick retrieval of previously learned words difficult.

Further brain imaging studies funded by the National Institute of Child Health and Human Development (NICHD) not only found there is a disruption in the brains of children who are struggling to learn how to read, but that, through good teaching, the brains of children with dyslexia begin to function more like the brains of children who have learned easily how to read. The children with dyslexia begin to show increased activation in the automatic recognition center (long-term memory area) of the brain.

This research has shown that children with dyslexia have trouble developing an awareness that words are made up of individual sounds (phonemes) and that print represent those sounds. By knowing that dyslexia is a language problem, we can better target teaching strategies that will help the dyslexic reader acquire the necessary phonological skills to become a successful reader.

Common Misunderstandings about Dyslexia

Writing letters and words backwards are symptoms of dyslexia.

This is not true. Writing letters and words backwards are common in early childhood and in the early stages of learning to read and write. This is true for all children—whether or not they have dyslexia. As a matter of fact, many children who should have been diagnosed with dyslexia in the early grades were not diagnosed until much later because they did not print letters or words with reversals.

More boys than girls have dyslexia.

This is not true. Studies show that as many girls as boys are affected by dyslexia. Boys may be identified as having dyslexia more often than girls due to reasons such as greater acting out behaviors in boys. Girls also seem to have the ability to compensate for their reading problems better than boys.

Visual perception problems can cause dyslexia.

This is not true. Research indicates that dyslexia is caused by a problem with language processing at the phoneme level.

Dyslexia only affects English-speaking people.

This is not true. Dyslexia occurs in all cultures in the world that have written languages. In English, the primary difficulty is with accurately decoding unknown words. In languages that have consistent orthographies—meaning grapheme-phoneme correspondences are mainly one-to-one—dyslexia appears more often as a fluency problem; a student's reading may be accurate, but very slow.

People with dyslexia will benefit from colored text overlays or lenses.

Studies do not show any strong evidence that the use of colored overlays or special lenses by dyslexic children has an effect on the ability to read words or comprehend text. However, a condition called scotopic sensitivity syndrome (SSS) can occur in up to 8 percent of people with dyslexia. SSS causes discomfort when working under bright or fluorescent lights, and causes problems with reading black text on white or gloss paper and perceiving print as shifting or blurring (see pages 78 and 79). Many parents of children with dyslexia have found it beneficial to use colored overlays or lenses—this may simply help children track text. More research is needed.

All children with dyslexia have attention-deficit/hyperactivity disorder (ADHD).

This is not true. Although ADHD is a separate condition, research has shown that as many as 40 percent of children who have dyslexia may also have ADHD.

Children will outgrow dyslexia.

Unfortunately, this is not true. There is no evidence that dyslexia can be outgrown. Instead, a child with reading problems will most likely continue to have difficulty with the ability to read.

A person with dyslexia can never learn to read.

This is simply not true. Research conducted by the National Institute of Child Health and Human Development indicates that the earlier children who are struggling to learn to read are identified and given systematic instruction, the less severe their reading problems are likely to be. Studies show that with good instruction, even older children with dyslexia can become accurate, if slow, readers.

Signs and Symptoms of Dyslexia

The majority of children with dyslexia are not identified until third grade or later. This is often due to the fact that these children are bright, verbal, and by all outward appearances, should be doing well in school. It is not until they are failing and falling significantly behind their peers that they are diagnosed.

Early identification is crucial. The earlier children with dyslexia are identified, the easier it is to remediate their problems. When a diagnosis occurs after third grade, a child's dyslexia is much more difficult to treat. Consequently, the observations of parents and preschool, kindergarten, and first grade teachers are crucial. There are many distinguishable warning signs during these early years that could alert you to those children who may have significant trouble learning how to read.

The following is a list of observable behaviors that children with dyslexia or other developmental reading disorders may exhibit. These are just some of the problems that can be observed in children who are at risk of reading failure.

The Earliest Sign

❑ **Family History**—Research has shown that between one-quarter to one-half of children born to a dyslexic parent will also have dyslexia. The earliest signs to look for are oral language difficulties. A child can be evaluated for dyslexia as early as age four.

Speech—Before Going to School

❑ **Delayed Speech**—Delays in speech can be subtle and go unnoticed or may be quite pronounced.

❑ **Immature Speech and/or Articulation Difficulties**—Immature speech is not uncommon among incoming kindergartners. However, there are specific signals that teachers can listen and look for, such as spoken words where letters (either beginning or ending sounds) are being dropped or when speech resembles "baby talk."

❑ **Poor Communication Skills**—These children may not be able to recall common vocabulary when asking for things or when expressing a need. They seem to lack general knowledge and often take a long time when trying to give or recall information.

❑ **Misheard Phonemes**—While speaking, the child will leave off beginning or ending sounds.

❑ **Substitution of Phonemes**—For example, the child may say *car* for *cap*—a word that makes no sense in context.

❑ **Mixing Up of Sounds in Multisyllabic Words**—For example, the child may say *aminal* for *animal*, *bisghetti* for *spaghetti*, or *hangaburger* for *hamburger*.

Other Observable Early Learning Behaviors

❑ **Preference to Not Sit and Listen to Stories**—The child would rather ramble or move from activity to activity.

❑ **Difficulty in Sequencing Story Events**—When listening to a story, the child will either miss or rearrange key events.

❑ **Poorly Developed Fine Motor Skills**—These skills are noticeably less mature than the majority of other children who are the same age. For example, they include far fewer details in their drawings. Children might also have difficulty learning how to tie their shoes.

❑ **Lack of Interest in Nursery Rhymes and Rhyming Words**—This can signal an inability to hear phonemes. The child may not comprehend that words can be separated into individual sounds.

❑ **Confusion of Positional, Directional, and Basic Concepts**—For example, the child may confuse concepts such as right and left, up and down, and yesterday and tomorrow.

❑ **Confusion with Left- and Right-Handedness**—The child may switch from the right hand to the left hand while coloring, writing, or performing any task. Eventually, the child will decide on a dominant hand but may prefer to use one hand for writing and the other for athletic activities.

 Teaching Tips for Kids with Dyslexia

Early Signs in School

- **Failure to Understand that Words Come Apart**—This underdeveloped skill prevents children from understanding that words like *snowman* can be broken down into the two words, *snow* and *man*. Later, they will not grasp that, for example, the three phonemes /m/, /a/, and /n/ blend together to make the word *man*.

- **Difficulty in Learning the Names and Sounds of Alphabet Letters**—This underdeveloped skill prevents children from "sounding out" unknown words and being able to connect a letter, such as d, with the sound /d/.

- **Lack of Awareness of Sounds and Sequence**—The child is unable to distinguish and separate phonemes in spoken words or identify the order of the sounds and the sequence of syllables.

- **Difficulty with Decoding Small Words**—These children struggle with the correspondence of sounds to letters when spelling words and may not even be able to sound out and spell simple three-letter, consonant-vowel-consonant words (for example, *hen, men, mat, cat, log,* or *dog*).

Later Signs in School

- **Continuation of Speech Problems**—The child mispronounces large words, either leaving out part of the word or confusing the order of the word parts. Speech may not be fluent; the child may hesitate, stammer, or simply appear to need extra time in responding. The child may also not be able to recall specific words or may make up new words, such as *widewind* for *whirlwind*.

- **Difficulty with Recognizing Small Sight Words**—The child is unable to recall small functional words such as *it, in, I, me, the, was,* and *to.*

- **Difficulty with Reading New Words**—The child may seem unable to use any decoding strategies.

- **Omission of Word Parts when Reading**—The child may read *helicopter* as *helopter.*

- **Oral Reading without Fluency**—The child's reading is not smooth, but choppy and slow.

- **Difficulty with Comprehension**—Because the child spends so much time on figuring out what the words are, much of a text's meaning is lost.

- **Difficulty with Timely Completion**—These children may struggle with completing tests in the allotted time and homework assignments seem to go on forever.

- **Great Difficulty with Spelling**—The child may lack recognition of letter-sound associations, patterns in words, syllables, and meaningful words parts.

- **Discrepancy between Performance and Ability**—The child's apparent intellectual ability is far above his actual reading and school achievements.

- **Difficulty with Handwriting**—Even though other fine motor skills might be good, such as typing or playing athletics, the child's handwriting appears messy and immature.

- **Complaints that Reading Is Too Hard**—Some children may express frustration or may even begin to feel ill at reading time.

Strengths of People with Dyslexia

It is extremely important to look for each child's strengths. Understanding a child's strengths better enables you to plan direct-instruction lessons that have a higher probability of attaining success. A child with dyslexia or with a developmental reading disorder typically has average to above-average intelligence. This reading disability is a language processing problem and is NOT connected to the ability to think or to comprehend complex higher-order thinking.

As reviewed in the section on Dyslexia and Current Brain Research (pages 5 and 6), these children simply have brains that are "wired" a little differently, creating unique learning styles. While dyslexia may present certain challenges, it is also associated with many talents and strengths. For example:

> ❏ **Dyslexic children are often creative thinkers and highly imaginative and may excel in drama, art, or music.**
>
> ❏ **Many dyslexic children have superior reasoning abilities that can be observed when they play games of strategy, build with construction materials, and solve complicated puzzles.**
>
> ❏ **Dyslexic children often have a high-level of understanding if new concepts are read to them. This skill also enables them to acquire a large listening vocabulary.**

Instead of viewing dyslexia or developmental reading disorders simply as disabilities, also view them as individual learning styles. All children have different learning styles, unique strengths, and varying ways that they perceive, organize, conceptualize, and recall information.

Using a multisensory approach that combines visual, auditory, and tactile experiences will simultaneously provide all of the children in a class with the opportunity to utilize their most dominant learning styles. This instructional method, along with systematic sequential phonics, will provide all children the most comprehensive reading experience.

Multisensory activities that involve seeing, speaking, listening, and touching are designed to help children learn to read faster—not only children who are struggling, but all of the children in your classroom.

Famous People with Dyslexia

Scott Adams–comic strip creator	Henry Ford–inventor	Carl Lewis– Olympic athlete
Hans Christian Andersen–writer	Benjamin Franklin–inventor	Michelangelo–artist
Alexander Graham Bell–inventor	Magic Johnson–athlete	Jack Nicholson–actor
Terry Bradshaw–football player	Whoopi Goldberg–actor	Pablo Picasso–artist
Prince Charles–English royalty	John Grisham–writer	Edgar Allen Poe–writer
Cher–singer/actor	Woody Harrelson–actor	Patricia Polacco–children's writer
Agatha Christie–writer	Tommy Hilfiger–designer	Charles Schulz–comic strip creator
Tom Cruise–actor	Dustin Hoffman–actor	Mark Twain–writer
Leonardo da Vinci–artist	Anthony Hopkins–actor	Jules Verne–writer
Walt Disney–producer	Bruce Jenner–Olympic athlete	Robin Williams–actor
Thomas Edison–inventor	Jewel–musician	Henry Winkler–actor
Albert Einstein–inventor/scientist	John Lennon–musician	Orville and Wilbur Wright–inventors
Dwight Eisenhower–U.S. President	Jay Leno–entertainer	

Diagnosis and Assessments

Parents and teachers are generally the first people to suspect that a child is having, or is going to have, a problem learning to read. Parents should first seek the advice of their child's pediatrician; a checkup, including a full health history and a vision and hearing evaluation, will rule out any medical or physical problems that are interfering with the child's learning abilities. A school psychologist and reading specialist can be consulted for further evaluations. A battery of assessments will be used to discover the specific difficulties associated with dyslexia and to suggest appropriate educational interventions.

Comprehensive Test of Phonological Processing (CTOPP) Wagner, Torgesen, and Rashotte (PRO-ED, Inc. © 1999). The CTOPP assesses phonological awareness, phonological memory, and rapid naming, quickly identifying individuals who may have reading problems due to weak phonological skills.

Gray Oral Reading Tests, Fourth Edition (GORT-4) Wiederholt and Bryant (PRO-ED, Inc. © 2001). The GORT-4 measures oral reading rate, accuracy, fluency, and comprehension. After the child reads a series of passages aloud, the child's oral reading is scored for rate and accuracy.

Lindamood Auditory Conceptualization Test (LAC-3) Lindamood and Lindamood (PRO-ED, Inc. © 2004). The LAC-3 is an individually administered, norm-referenced assessment that measures an individual's ability to perceive and conceptualize speech sounds using a visual medium. The LAC-3 also measures the cognitive ability to distinguish and manipulate sounds.

The Phonological Awareness Assessment Instrument (Found in the book *Phonemic Awareness in Young Children: A Classroom Curriculum* by Marilyn Adams, et al. Brookes Publishing © 1998). This test assesses students in six areas of phonological and phonemic awareness: detecting rhymes, counting syllables, matching initial sounds, counting phonemes, comparing word lengths, and representing phonemes with letters.

The Phonological Awareness Test 2 (PAT) Robertson and Salter (LinguiSystems, Inc. © 2007). The PAT measures students' (second semester kindergarten through second grade) ability on five phonemic awareness tasks: segmentation, isolation, deletion, substitution, and blending, as well as sensitivity to rhyme, knowledge of graphemes, and decoding skills.

Rosner Test of Auditory Analysis Skills (TAAS) Rosner (Academic Therapy © 1979). The TAAS tests oral word analysis skills with 13 single word phonetic deletion items. Test takers are given words orally and asked to delete a beginning sound, an ending sound, or a part of a blend.

TOPA-2+ Test of Phonological Awareness Second Edition: Plus Torgesen and Bryant (LinguiSystems, Inc. © 2004). This is a group–administered, norm-referenced measure of phonological awareness. There are two versions—kindergarten and early elementary—that measure young children's abilities to isolate individual phonemes in spoken words and understand the relationships between letter and phonemes.

The Woodcock Reading Mastery Test—Revised (WRMT-R) Woodcock (American Guidance Service, 1998). The WRMT-R has two forms and includes these subtests: letter identification, word identification, nonsense words, word comprehension, and passage comprehension.

Yopp-Singer Test of Phoneme Segmentation (Yopp, H. K. *The Reading Teacher* 49 No. 1 [September, 1995]: 20–29). Designed to be used with English-speaking kindergartners, this test measures a student's ability to orally segment the phonemes in a word in their correct order.

Chapter Two
Getting Ready to Read—
Phonemic Awareness

Dr. Jeanne Chall, a leading expert in reading research and instruction, identified five stages of reading acquisition (Chall 1983, pgs. 13–24). In Chall's well-known model, each stage builds on skills mastered in earlier stages; a child's lack of mastery at any level can impede or even stop progress beyond that level.

It was stated earlier in this book that all children, even children with dyslexia, must go through each of the stages of reading. The majority of children with dyslexia begin their struggles in Stage 0 where they lack an awareness of sound similarities in words; for example, they do not demonstrate an understanding of rhyming words or alliteration of initial phonemes. Building a strong foundation in the area of prereading will greatly assist the young child with dyslexia in moving through the other stages of reading.

Chall's Stages of Reading Development

❏ **Stage 0. Prereading:** Typically achieved by age six, children grow in familiarity with the language and its sounds, gaining insights into the nature of words: some words sound similar at their beginnings or endings, and words can be broken into parts and the parts can be put together to create whole words. Children begin to recognize a few familiar written words. Chall's Stage 0 is often called *reading readiness* and is required for an optimal transition into beginning reading.

❏ **Stage 1. Initial reading stage, or decoding stage:** Developing readers typically reach this stage by the age of six or seven. The learner becomes aware of the correspondence between sounds and letters. As this knowledge is applied to text, the reader demonstrates an understanding of the critical concept of the alphabetic principle and is using sound-symbol relationships—the *alphabetic system*.

❏ **Stage 2. Confirmation:** Usually reached by the age of seven or eight, the reader consolidates what was learned in Stage 1. The reader does not read to gain new information but to confirm what is already known. As decoding skills continue to improve, the reader begins to develop fluency and speed in addition to accuracy in word recognition, giving attention both to meaning and to the print. In this critical stage, the beginning reader must have the opportunity of reading many familiar books.

❏ **Stage 3. Reading to learn:** This stage usually begins in fourth grade around the age of nine and continues to age fourteen. Here, the task changes from mastering the print to the mastering of ideas as the reader begins to use reading skills to gain information. The reader learns how to learn from reading. The development of vocabulary also accelerates at this stage.

❏ **Stage 4. Multiple viewpoints:** These skills are typically developed during high school from ages 14 to 19. Readers at this stage begin to deal with layers of facts and concepts, understand different points of view, and react critically to what they read.

❏ **Stage 5. Construction and judgement:** Not usually reached until college age or later, readers at this highest stage have learned to read selectively—knowing what not to read as well as what to read. They form their own opinions about what they have read and, using analysis, synthesis, and judgement, they construct their knowledge from that of others.

To further your knowledge of how children learn to read, it is necessary to understand that the English language is an **alphabetic system**—it uses written characters or symbols **(graphemes)** to represent sounds **(phonemes)** and sound patterns. However, it is not just a phonetic system. It is also an **orthographic** or spelling system that reflects **meaning** rather than just sounds. It is based primarily on the assumption that each speech sound or **phoneme** should have its own graphic representation. When a child develops an awareness of the relationship between sounds and letters and then begins to apply that knowledge to text, he is understanding the concept of the **alphabetic principle**.

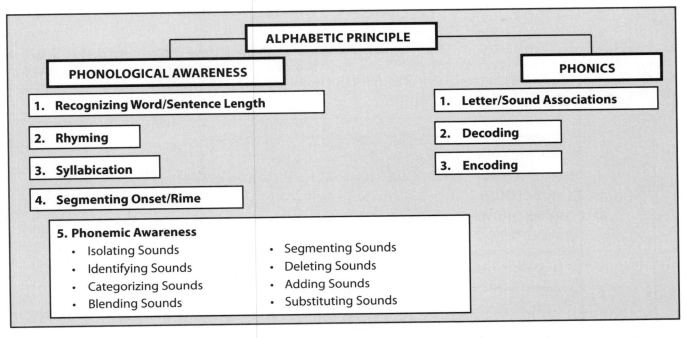

According to the National Reading Panel (NRP), the ability to read requires proficiency in phonemic awareness, phonics, fluency, vocabulary, and text comprehension. Following are definitions of these terms:

❑ **Phonemic awareness** is the ability to focus on and manipulate the individual sounds of spoken syllables and words. The broader term, phonological awareness, includes larger parts of spoken language such as words, syllables, and onsets and rimes. It also includes rhyming and syllabication.

❑ **Phonics** is a form of instruction that stresses the acquisition of letter-sound correspondences. It cultivates the understanding of how letters are linked to sounds (phonemes), that letters represent those sounds in written language, and how to apply this knowledge to decode words.

❑ **Fluency** is the ability to read a text orally with speed, accuracy, and proper vocal expression and comprehension. Because fluent readers do not have to concentrate on decoding words, they can focus on the meaning of the ideas expressed in the text and relate them to their background knowledge.

❑ **Vocabulary** simply refers to the words a reader knows. Vocabulary development is a critical aspect of reading comprehension. A reader must try to decode an unfamiliar word and determine its spoken pronunciation to know if the word is in the reader's oral vocabulary. If it is not, the reader must try to determine the word's meaning using another strategy, such as context.

❑ **Text comprehension** is understanding what is read. The reader, in a complex cognitive process, intentionally and interactively engages with the text. Readers comprehend text when they employ intentional, problem-solving thinking processes, relating ideas found in the print to their own knowledge and experiences.

What Phonemic Awareness Is and Why It Is So Important in Learning How to Read

We have seen in the preceding pages that phonemic awareness is the ability to work with individual sounds, or phonemes, in spoken words. Phonemes are the smallest units of spoken—not written— language. Each child needs to understand that spoken words are made up of sounds and that new words can be created by combining, blending, and separating those sounds. The skill of phonemic awareness must be taught and developed before children can learn to read.

Phonemic awareness is the first true step in learning how to read and is the skill that children with dyslexia as well as other reading disabilities have the most difficult time acquiring. Children who are unable to hear the phonemes in spoken words and cannot understand how a sequence of sounds forms individual words will, in all likelihood, have a difficult time equating specific sounds to the corresponding letters.

Children lacking phonemic awareness will struggle with the following tasks:

❏ **Rhyming:** How many words can you rhyme with the word *cat*?

❏ **Phoneme Matching:** Do the words *dog* and *duck* begin with the same sound?

❏ **Phoneme Counting:** How many sounds do you hear in the word *bike*?

❏ **Phoneme Blending:** What word do you hear when you put the sounds /p/ /i/ /g/ together?

❏ **Phoneme Segmentation:** What is the last sound in the word *cap*? What sounds do you hear in the word *bed*?

❏ **Phoneme Deletion:** What word would you have if /p/ was taken away from the word *pin*?

❏ **Phoneme Addition:** What word would you have if /k/ was added to the word *lap*?

❏ **Phoneme Substitution:** What word would you have if you changed /m/ in *men* to /h/?

Phonemic awareness instruction benefits all children; however, effective instruction in phonemic awareness skills may actually make the difference between reading success and reading failure for over 20 percent of children.

Prephonemic Awareness, Sound Awareness, and Listening Skills

Phonemic awareness skills can and must be taught to children who lack these skills. To begin this instruction, help children become more observant of everyday sounds. Their heightened awareness of how environmental sounds differ will also help them discern and learn to identify speech sounds in oral language. Throughout the day, there will be many learning opportunities for children to talk about sounds that are generated in the classroom or at home or noises that happen outside. Be sure to help children recall the sounds they have heard during group time, transition time, rest time, snack time, and on walks in the neighborhood. The following prephonemic awareness and listening activities also target alertness, discrimination, and memory skills.

Everyday Sounds

During group time, distribute two or three common objects and/or musical instruments to each child while the children sit on the floor in a circle. Allow the group a few minutes to explore what sounds they can make with their materials. Then, direct children to arrange their noisemakers on the floor in a special way. (This helps the children to "turn off" the noisemakers.) Begin the activity by asking children to make very soft sounds and then ask them to make sounds that are louder. Talk about the materials they used to make the sounds and what they did to change the dynamics. Continue the activity by choosing a child to be a noisemaker. Direct the remaining children to cover their eyes and listen carefully for a sound that will be made by the chosen child. The noisemaker then selects one of the instruments, walks to another part of the classroom, and makes a soft sound behind a large object. Have the children uncover their eyes. Ask: "Where is the noisemaker?" and "What did the noisemaker use to make the noise?" Continue as time and interest allow.

Identify a Missing Sound

This activity is similar to the activity Everyday Sounds (page 14). This time have children close their eyes while you make a series of sounds, such as tapping a pencil, walking in place, and snapping fingers. Repeat the series of sounds but omit one of them. The children must identify which sound is missing.

This game can become more challenging by asking children to identify the sounds in the order in which they were heard or by asking the children questions, such as, "What sound did you hear first? Which sound was second? What was the last sound you heard?"

What Do You Hear? Big Book

Share with the children some stories about hearing and sounds, such as *Polar Bear, Polar Bear What Do You Hear?* by Bill Martin Jr. (Henry Holt, 1992). Ask each child to name something she has heard, such as popcorn popping, a bird singing, a dog barking, a fire truck siren, etc. Then, ask children to create illustrations of the objects or animals they heard. Bind all of the pictures together to make a classroom big book of sounds. Write on the top of each page, "(*Child's name, child's name), *what did you hear?" At the bottom of the page write, "I heard a *(child's response)."* The children will enjoy "reading" their classroom big book of sounds over and over again.

Polar Bear, Polar Bear What Do You Hear?

Who's Talking?—1

Ask children to sit anywhere they want in the classroom. First, play this game with the children's eyes open so that they understand how the game works. Then, ask them to close their eyes and promise not to peek. Walk quietly around the classroom and tap one child on the shoulder. The tapped child says, "*(Another child's name)* where am I?" The named child calls out, "You are *(first child's name),"* and then describes where the first child is located.

Who's Talking?—2

Ask the children to sit in a circle. Choose one child to sit in the middle of the circle with his eyes closed. Walk around the circle and tap another child on the shoulder. That child says a silly sentence such as, "The cow jumped over the moon." The child in the center of the circle must guess who said the silly sentence.

Noisemakers

Ask the children to bring something to class that could be made into a noisemaker. Send home a note to parents explaining the activity. Include suggestions such as rice, dried peas, pebbles, beans, empty and clean plastic bottles, containers with lids (for example, margarine or yogurt containers), and small boxes (for example, oatmeal or jewelry boxes).

Let children create their own noisemakers. They should color their containers and fill them with noise-making objects. Help children seal the containers with tape. Let each child explain to the class how her noisemaker was made, describe what is inside the noisemaker, and demonstrate its sound by shaking it. Conclude the lesson by having children become a band and play along with a favorite musical recording.

Loud and Soft

Use a xylophone or bells. Demonstrate the dynamics of loud and soft sounds and then ask children to take turns creating loud or soft sounds with the musical instruments. Next, have children stand in a line and listen very carefully. Play a sound. Tell children if the next sound they hear is louder, they should take a step forward. If the second sound is softer, they should take a step backwards.

Beginning, Middle, Ending, and Changing Sounds

This is a great activity to help children understand that sounds can be in a specific position and that sounds can be manipulated. Place three different animal pictures on a chalkboard ledge or chart stand. Ask children which animal is first, which is in the middle, and which one is last. Switch the arrangement of the animals and repeat the question to practice these concepts. Next, choose three instruments and make three distinct sounds. Ask children which sound they heard first, which sound was in the middle, and which was last. Invite a child to make three more sounds to continue the activity.

Recognizing Specific Sounds and Words

In this activity, children will listen for a particular word or sound. Read a favorite nursery rhyme, short story, or poem. Then, ask children to raise their hands each time they hear a predetermined sound or word. For example, in the rhyme, "Twinkle, Twinkle, Little Star," ask children to raise their hands each time they hear the word *little*.

Variation: Have children raise their hands each time they hear an incorrect word (for example, twinkle, twinkle, *bigger* star) or a nonsense word.

Rhyming Activities

Being aware of and recognizing rhyming words is a necessary step in learning to read. As young children become cognizant of the predictable language in books, such as *Brown Bear, Brown Bear, What Do You See?* by Bill Martin Jr. and illustrated by Eric Carle (Henry Holt and Company, 1992), they also begin to notice that certain words rhyme, for example, "Brown bear, brown bear, what do you *see*? I see a red bird looking at *me*." As you read aloud the remainder of the book, emphasize the rhyming words so that children's awareness of rhyme becomes sharper. In addition, as you foster this skill, select texts that feature common phonograms because the next step for emerging readers is to make the connection that some rhyming words end with the same letters.

Clapping and Snapping Games

Playing rhyming games and singing rhyming songs help children learn to pay attention to the sounds in words. Many songs and games include clapping, snapping fingers, bouncing, and tossing balls or beanbags. For example, combine rhythm and rhyming words with this pattern: clap, clap, snap (say, "cat"), clap, clap, snap (say, "hat"), clap, clap, snap (say, "rat"). Using real words is not important—what is important is that the spoken words rhyme with the other words.

Rhyming Word "Jump-Up"

Have children walk around the classroom. Say two words. When children hear a pair of words that rhyme, they jump up!

Name Games

Children love playing games that use their names.

Assign silly names. Children think this game is very silly. Look at one child, for example, "Nate" and call him "Tate." Then, look at "Katie" and call her "Matie." Let children have fun thinking of new rhyming names for each other.

Sing "The Name Game." It is also fun to teach children a song based on "The Name Game" by Shirley Elliston and Lincoln Chase (1964 EMI Al Gallico Music Corp.). Here are two examples to get you going: Sherry, Sherry, Bo-Berry, Fee-Fi-Fo-Ferry, Sherry; Danny, Danny, Bo-Banny, Fe-Fi-Fo-Fanny, Danny.

Give Willoughby Wallaby names. This delightful song based on a poem by Dennis Lee was recorded by Raffi on *Singable Songs for the Very Young* (1996 Rounder/UMGD). Children will love generating new rhyming names, for example, Willoughby Wallaby Wecca, an elephant sat on Becca.

"Down by the Bay"

The traditional song "Down by the Bay," also recorded by Raffi (see above), is an excellent song for helping children become more aware of words that rhyme. Let children listen to and learn the words before introducing the concept of identifying the words in each refrain that rhyme. Give each child a musical instrument. Let them "make music" each time they hear a rhyming word.

Let Loose—with Seuss and the Goose!

Mother Goose and Dr. Seuss probably never knew the positive impact their rhymes were going to have on teaching phonemic awareness. Besides simply enjoying their delightful rhymes, children can participate in specific activities that focus on rhyming patterns. (See Children's Books and Songs to Increase Phonemic Awareness on pages 45 and 46.) The five activities below can be completed with any nursery rhyme or any story that contains rhyming words.

- ❏ **Fill in the blank.** Read a familiar rhyme. Then, explain to children that you are going to read the rhyme again, but this time you will leave out some words. Pause at the end of a rhyming phrase and let children fill in the missing word, for example, "Jack and <u>Jill</u>, went up the _____."

- ❏ **Find new words.** Identify words that rhyme in the text (*Jill, hill*) and generate other rhyming words such as *pill, fill, dill*, and *Bill*.

- ❏ **Clap on the rhyme.** Clap every time a rhyming word is heard.

- ❏ **Create illustrations.** Have children illustrate pairs of rhyming words such as *Jill* and *hill*. Point out the illustrations in the book that depict the words that rhyme.

- ❏ **Make silly rhymes.** Review a traditional rhyme and then create a new silly rhyme. For example, review the rhyme, "Little Miss Muffet Sat on a Tuffet," and change the verse to "Little Brown Bear sat on a chair, eating a jar of honey. Along came a bee that flew onto his knee and said 'Where is my money?'"

More Advanced Rhyming Activities

Take the Train
Choose one child to be the engineer. As the engineer begins to walk around the room, he stops beside another child and says a word. That child must say a word that rhymes with the engineer's word. Then, the two children walk together in a line, stop beside another child, and say a new word to rhyme. The game keeps going until everyone has joined the train.

Rhyming Pairs Memory Match—Page 18
Enlarge and copy, color, and cut out the rhyming picture cards on page 18. Lay the cards facedown on a table. Children should say the words aloud as they look and listen for the rhyming matches.

Parrot Talk
Parrots usually mimic what is said, but this "parrot" is confused. He never says the word he hears; instead, he always says a word that rhymes. Let the children take turns being the "parrot" and the "parrot's owner."

Smiling-Face Lollipops
Provide each child with a yellow construction paper smiling face attached to a craft stick. Say pairs of words. If the two words rhyme, the children hold up their smiling-face lollipops.

Wrong Word
Show children a set of three or four pictures. The children must decide which word for one of the pictures in the set does not rhyme with the others. As a variation, show children two pictures with names that do not rhyme. Then, say a word, and the child must choose the picture with the name that rhymes with that word. For example, show pictures of a hat and a box and say the word *fox*. The child would choose the picture of the rhyming word *box*.

Ideas for Older Children—Page 19
Keeping activities age appropriate, use raps, slogans, commercials, and T-shirt sayings for rhyming practice. Reproduce the T-shirt pattern found on page 19 for children to use as they practice writing their own T-shirt rhymes.

The Best Word Families and Rhyming Words for Beginners

–ag: bag, nag, rag, sag, tag, wag, brag, drag, flag	**–ell:** bell, cell, fell, Nell, sell, tell, well, yell, shell, smell, spell	**–ock:** dock, hock, knock, lock, rock, sock, block, clock, flock, shock
–all: ball, call, fall, hall, mall, tall, wall, small, stall	**–en:** Ben, den, hen, Ken, men, pen, ten, then, when	**–ook:** book, cook, hook, look, nook, took, brook, shook
–ame: came, fame, game, lame, name, same, tame, blame, frame	**–et:** bet, get, jet, let, met, net, pet, set, wet, yet, fret	**–op:** bop, cop, hop, mop, pop, top, chop, drop, shop, stop
–an: ban, can, Dan, fan, man, pan, ran, tan, van, plan, than	**–ick:** Dick, kick, lick, Nick, pick, quick, Rick, sick, tick, wick, brick, stick, trick	**–ot:** cot, dot, got, hot, lot, not, pot, rot, tot, plot, spot
–and: and, band, hand, land, sand, brand, stand	**–ig:** big, dig, fig, jig, pig, rig, wig, twig	**–uck:** buck , duck, luck, muck, puck, tuck, Chuck, pluck, truck
–at: at, bat, cat, fat, mat, nat, rat, sat, chat, brat, that	**–ill:** bill, dill, fill, gill, hill, ill, Jill, kill, mill, pill, quill, sill, will, chill, drill, grill, spill	**–ug:** bug, dug, hug, jug, mug, pug, rug, tug, plug, slug, snug
–eat: beat, eat, feat, heat, meat, neat, seat, cheat, treat	**–ine:** dine, fine, line, mine, nine, pine, vine, shine, spine, whine	**–ump:** bump, dump, hump, jump, lump, pump, rump, grump, stump
–ed: bed, fed, led, Ned, red, Ted, wed, bled, fled, Fred, sled	**–ing:** bing, ding, king, ping, ring, sing, wing, bring, sting, swing, thing	
–eed: deed, feed, heed, need, reed, seed, weed, bleed, freed, speed	**–ip:** dip, hip, lip, nip, rip, sip, tip, zip, chip, drip, flip, ship, trip	

Reproducible Rhyming Pictures

Pictures: *cat–hat, pig–wig, hen–ten, run–sun, block–clock, chair–hair, bee–tree, car–star*

(Directions are found on page 17.)

  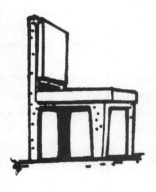 

Reproducible T-Shirt Pattern

(Directions are found on page 17.)

Word Awareness

Thus far, we have seen the importance and necessity of building sound awareness by developing good listening skills. These skills help children learn to attend to and distinguish both environmental sounds and speech sounds from one another. After developing sound awareness, children learn to identify rhyming words and understand that words that rhyme have identical final sounds. The next important building block for learning how to read is to acquire **word awareness**. Children achieve word awareness when they understand that sentences consist of words and that these words can be manipulated.

According to Dr. Candace Goldsworthy, professor of speech-language pathology at California State University, Sacramento, word awareness is the first level of language analysis and must occur before children can begin the task of segmenting words into phonemes—the smallest sound components. When word awareness is first introduced to children, it is best to use content words (nouns) such as *bike*, *house*, *boy*, and *dog*. Children seem to more readily understand that these are individual words, rather than using words such as *the*, *and*, *at*, and *it*. Using content words in simple sentences will promote and strengthen children's understanding of the concept of word awareness.

Beginning Word Awareness Activities

Singing Exciting Songs

Sing songs that accentuate single words or have simple repetitive phrases, such as "Row, row, row your boat," "London bridge is falling down, falling down, falling down," or "Skip, skip, skip to my Lou."

Reading Stories Aloud

❏ **Point to the words.** Big books are wonderful to use when beginning to introduce word awareness. As you read aloud, point to each word. After the children have become familiar with the content of the story, let them take turns pointing to the words as you read them.

❏ **Fill in the missing words.** As you read a familiar story, stop and let the children fill in missing words. For example, when reading the book, *One Fish, Two Fish, Red Fish, Blue Fish* by Dr. Seuss, read the title as *One Fish, _____ Fish, Red Fish, _____ Fish.* Children should supply the words *Two* and *Blue.* Praise the children and tell them that they supplied the words that were needed.

❏ **What's the next word?** Pause on occasion when reading and pointing to the words in a big book and let the children "read" one of the words. Prompt the children by pausing and then saying, "What word is next?"

Counting Words

First, practice counting with the children. Count how many children are in the class or how many windows are in the classroom. Next, explain that now you are going to count words.

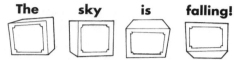

Use familiar nursery rhymes or fairy tales so that children are already familiar with the content and the words used in the selection. For example, say, "How many words do you hear in this sentence? 'The sky is falling!'" The children would answer, "four." Or, use the wolf's phrase, "I'll huff and I'll puff." Children would then count five words.

Variation: To provide children with a more concrete experience, give each child five or six blocks. Have the children move a block forward for each word they hear. Then, have them repeat the sentence with you—touching a block for each word. Finally, count the blocks to "see" how many words were in the sentence.

—— Increase the Difficulty as Children Develop Word Awareness ——

Story Dictation

Many children with dyslexia have excellent comprehension of the stories that have been read or told to them; large vocabularies that often surpass their peers in the same age group; and vivid and creative imaginations. Original story dictation is an excellent tool for utilizing the strengths of these children and for inspiring their motivation to want to learn to read.

❏ **Dictate short high-interest stories.** Choose a story topic that you know will interest your students. Encourage students to generate sentences to create a story on the topic. Write the story sentences on chart paper or sentence strips. Be sure to write the words in exactly the same way the children say them. At first, keep the stories to four or five sentences, writing one sentence per line.

❏ **Learn about sentences.** This is the perfect time to introduce the concept of a sentence. Each time you write a sentence, clearly identify it as a sentence. It is also not too early to point out that the first word in the sentence begins with a "tall" or uppercase letter and that the sentence ends with a "dot" or period. Children will also notice that, as you write and read the words, you are moving from left to right.

❏ **Fix mixed-up sentences.** Make sure children are comfortable with the original story you recorded as they dictated sentences. Then, place the sentence strips out of order in the chart stand and read the new version of the story back to the children. The mixed-up story will undoubtedly not make much sense. Invite children to talk about why the story doesn't make sense. Then, have them rearrange the sentence strips into their original order so that their story once again makes sense.

—— When Children Are Beginning to Recognize Words ——

Sentence Segmentation

This is a difficult task, but it is included in this section because sometimes children who have not yet begun to phonetically decode words may actually recognize whole words from activities like story dictation (see above).

Take the sentence strips children created during a story dictation (which should be sentences they know well) and cut each sentence into individual words. Give one cut-up sentence to a group of children. Have children rearrange the words back into the original sentence and glue them onto another sentence strip. When the groups are finished, have each group read their sentence. Then, let the children decide which sentence came first in the story, which sentence was second, and so on until the original dictated story has been put back together in the correct order.

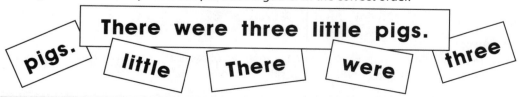

Recognizing Syllables

Now that children are aware of words as a whole they need to realize that words are made up of units of sound called syllables. This is another important listening skill that can actually start to develop when children begin to blend onsets and rimes to make words. Syllables, as larger units of sound, can be easier to hear and identify than the individual phonemes in words.

Singing and Saying Compound Words with Two Beats

For a fun and easy way to introduce the concept of syllables, have children sing the following song and say simple compound words that have two beats. Children who are familiar with this song will quickly say the word to the beat of the music instead of clapping at the end of each line. Tell children what word to say or have them supply compound words to use when singing the song. Examples include:

airplane	backyard	bedtime	birthday	corncob	football	mailbox	rooftop	snowball
anthill	bathtub	beehive	bookmark	doghouse	goldfish	notebook	sailboat	starfish
backdoor	beanbag	birdcage	bulldog	doorbell	haircut	popcorn	seagull	upstairs
backpack	bedroom	birdhouse	classroom	downhill	homework	rainbow	sidewalk	

If You Know a Compound Word, Say It Now!
(Sung to the tune of "If You're Happy and You Know It")
If you know a compound word, say it now. *(cupcake)*
If you know a compound word, say it now. *(cupcake)*
If you know a compound word, then your voice can say it loud.
If you know a compound word, say it now. *(cupcake!)*

Syllable Shakers

Have all of the children make their own syllable shakers. Use clean yogurt or margarine containers with lids and fill them partway with dried split green peas or rice to make noisemakers. Secure the lid with duct tape or shipping tape. Copy the syllable picture cards found on page 22. Print the numerals 1, 2, 3, and 4 individually on four pieces of
and lay the number cards on the table. Place the pictures cards facedown in a pile in the center of the playing area. Have children take turns drawing a card, saying the name of the picture on the card, and then repeating the name while shaking the container once for each syllable. Have the other players count the shakes and say their answers. Then, the child should place the picture next to the correct number card to show the number of syllables in the picture's name.

Variation: Read aloud a favorite picture book and select words from the text that have two or more syllables. Choose children to tell you how many beats (syllables) they hear when you say the words. To help them hear the syllables, encourage children to use their shakers when pronouncing the words.

Segmenting Syllables

Teaching syllable segmentation is important because children must learn that words are comprised of multiple sounds. Here are some activities to help children make this connection:

1. **Clap the syllables.** Clapping out the number of syllables allows children to really hear how words have multiple sounds. Children especially enjoy clapping the syllables in their own names.

2. **Count 'em:** After children clap each syllable in a word, ask them how many syllables they heard. Write the number down.

3. **Choose a syllable surprise.** Fill a small bag with common classroom items. Let children take turns picking an item out of the bag. Say the name of the item and then clap and count the syllables.

Reproducible Syllable Picture Cards

(Directions are found on page 21.)

Introducing and Isolating Phonemes

The next logical instructional step after children demonstrate proficiency in identifying rhyming words and recognizing syllables is to help them recognize individual sounds in words *(phoneme isolation)* and be able to recognize the same sounds in different words *(phoneme identity)*.

It is advisable to follow these steps when teaching phonemes:

❑ First, teach the 16 consonants that have only one phoneme (**b, d, f, h, j, k, l, m, n, p, q, r, t, v, x, z**).

❑ Then, introduce those letters that have more than one sound (**c, g, s, w, y**).

❑ Next, add each vowel by introducing both of its sounds (**long and short**).

❑ Finally, add the digraphs that have two letters that create one sound (**th, wh, ch, sh**).

Introducing Phonemes

Introduce phonemes with pictures *(visual clues)*; sound associations *(auditory clues)*, for example, teach children the Campbell's soup commercial—"M'm! M'm! Good!®" for /m/; use a metronome or ticking clock for /t/; make a buzzing sound, "zzzz" for /z/; and, gestures or movements *(kinesthetic clues)*. The multisensory experience of visualizing pictures, using auditory clues (songs, rhymes, chants, etc.), and kinesthetic experiences can significantly help these children learn to discriminate and isolate the phonemes—which will later help them make the connections between sounds and printed letters. (See pages 48–49 for ideas on visual, auditory, and kinesthetic methods for teaching letters.)

Looking in the Mirror

Let children watch themselves in a mirror as they say new sounds.

Same Sounds—Alliteration

When children listening to a story have a breakthrough and start to recognize strings of words that begin with the same initial phoneme, you know that they are using their listening skills to detect finer differences in sounds. Many sentences in picture books and nursery rhymes feature names or groupings of two or more words that begin with the same sounds. This literary element is called *alliteration*.

It is very easy to include some experiences with alliteration in the curriculum by choosing rhymes for children to hear and recite anytime throughout the day. To make a listening activity fun during transition time, choose an alliterative name or phrase and change the wording of the rhyme if necessary. Then, direct children to stop and listen for your "magic word(s)" while you recite the rhyme. When they hear the magic word(s), they can then move to the new location.

❑ Little Tommy Tittlemouse lived in a little house; . . .

❑ Daffy-Down-Dilly has now come to town . . .

❑ Diddlety, diddlety, dumpty, the cat ran up the plum tree; . . .

❑ Peter Piper picked a peck of pickled peppers; . . .

❑ Lucy Locket lost her pocket, Kitty Fisher found it; . . .

❑ Diddle diddle dumpling, my son John went to bed with his trousers on; . . .

❑ Pease porridge hot, pease porridge cold, . . .

❑ Sing a song of sixpence, a pocket full of rye; . . .

❑ Wee Willie Winkie runs through the town, . . .

❑ Fiddle-de-dee, fiddle-de-dee, the fly shall marry the bumblebee. . . .

Tongue Twisters and Literature—Listening Carefully to Reading Aloud

While you are reading aloud, have children listen carefully for specific phonemes. To assist them, accentuate the phoneme you want them to identify. Use tongue twisters that feature the specific phoneme the children are learning. (Tongue twister books can be found in the list of Children's Books and Songs to Increase Phonemic Awareness on pages 45 and 46.)

Small CVC Words—Stretching the Individual Sounds

Begin by having children analyze words with the CVC structure (consonant-vowel-consonant pattern). Choose a CVC word and then say it out loud to the children. If possible, prolong or stretch out the initial consonant sound, for example, say *man* as /mmmm/-an. Ask students to tell you the beginning sound in the word. Continue in the same manner with other chosen words. When children can recognize, isolate, and pronounce beginning consonant sounds, build on this skill by talking about and identifying the final sounds in simple words.

"Ducks-in-a-Line" (First, Middle, and Final Sounds)—Page 25

Make a copy of the Ducks-in-a-Line Patterns on page 25 for each child. Have children color their ducks and then cut them out. Help children arrange their ducks by explaining that ducks walk in a line. The mother duck is first in line—she will stand for the first sound in a word. Then, the middle -sized duck will stand for the middle sound, and the little duck at the end of the line will stand for the final sound in a word. Ask various questions about the words while children answer the questions by pointing to the corresponding duck in their lines of ducks. For example, ask, "Where is the /d/ sound in *dog*?" Say the word again, sound by sound, /d/-/o/-/g/. Children should answer "The /d/ sound is at the beginning." Ask about the position of other sounds in CVC words, such as, "Where is the /n/ sound in *ten*, /t/-/e/-/n/?" or "Where is the /a/ sound in *cat*, /c/-/a/-/t/?"

Alternatively, announce that the ducks in their lines are hungry, and it would be very fun to feed them. Give each child three paper cups, one for each of their ducks, and a small bowl of cereal and/or dried fruit. Each time you ask a question about a word, the child places a cereal piece in the corresponding cup. At the end of the activity, invite children to enjoy eating the snacks with their ducks.

Following are some examples of words with two phonemes:

be	do	it	knee	row	sew	tea	toe
chew	few	hay	mow	sea	shoe	tie	we
day	is	key	my	see	shy	to	zoo

Following are some examples of words with three phonemes:

bad	man	tan	men	big	kid	cod	pod	fun
bag	map	tap	met	bin	kin	cop	pop	gum
bat	mat	van	net	bit	kip	cot	pot	hug
cab	nag	wag	peg	did	kit	dog	rob	hut
can	nap	yam	pen	dig	lid	dot	rod	jug
cap	pad	yap	pet	dim	lip	fog	rot	mud
cat	pan	bed	red	dip	lit	fox	sob	mug
dad	pat	beg	set	fig	pig	got	top	nut
fan	rag	bet	yet	fin	pin	hog	bud	pug
fat	ram	den	ten	fit	pip	hop	bug	pup
had	ran	fed	vet	fix	pit	hot	bun	rub
ham	rap	get	web	hid	rib	job	bus	rug
hat	rat	hen	wed	him	rid	log	but	run
jam	sad	jet	wet	hip	rig	lot	cub	sum
lad	sat	keg	yes	his	rim	mop	cup	sun
lap	tab	leg	bib	hit	bob	nod	cut	tub
mad	tag	let	bid	jig	cob	not	dug	tug

Ducks-in-a-Line Patterns

(Directions are found on page 24.)

Phonemes

Phonemes	Graphemes *(letter/s representing the most common spellings)*	Word Examples	Phoneme Pictures	Phoneme Movements and Hand Gestures
Consonant Sounds			picture with beginning sound	
/b/	b, bb	**b**all, ru**bb**er	ball	pretend to bounce a ball
/d/	d, dd,	**d**og, see**d**, a**dd**	dog	pretend to pet a dog
/f/	f, ff, ph	**f**ish, **ph**oto, hu**ff**	fish	wiggle hands like a swimming fish
/g/	g, gg	**g**oat, **g**o, pi**g**, e**gg**	goat	finger points away from self, (go away)
/h/	h	**h**ot, **h**orse,	horse	"too hot" wave hand in front of mouth
/j/	j, g, ge, dge	**j**ump, **g**iraffe, pa**ge**, e**dge**	jump rope	pretend to jump rope
/k/	c, k, ck	**c**at, **k**ey, ba**k**e, du**ck**	cat	pull fingers away from nose (cat whiskers)
/l/	l, ll	**l**amp, sea**l**, fi**ll**	lamp	pretend to lick a lollipop
/m/	m, mm, mb	**m**onkey, yu**mm**y, co**mb**	mouse	rub stomach "mmmmm" good
/n/	n, nn, kn, gn	**n**ose, pa**n**, **kn**ee, **gn**ome	nest	shake head "no"
/p/	p, pp	**p**ie, shee**p**, a**pp**le	pie	pretend to "pop" bubbles
/kw/	qu	**qu**ack, s**qu**irt	queen	move fingers together (quack like a duck)
/r/	r, rr, wr	**r**un, be**rr**y, **wr**ite	rabbit	make running motion with fingers
/s/	s, se, ss, c, ce, sc	**s**un, hou**se**, me**ss**, **c**ity, i**ce**, **sc**ene	sun	wiggle arm and hand like a snake
/t/	t, tt	**t**op, ca**t**, le**tt**er	top	move arm like a metronome (tick tock)
/v/	v, ve	**v**ase, o**v**er, ca**ve**	vase	pretend to vacuum
/w/	w	**w**ing, s**w**im	window	wave hand back and forth
/ks/ /gz/	x, ex	bo**x**, e**x**it	exit sign	cross fingers to make an "X"
/y/	y	**y**es, **y**ak	yo-yo	nod head "yes"
/z/	z, zz, ze, s, se, x	**z**ip, whi**zz**, free**ze**, wa**s**, tea**se**, **x**ylophone	zipper	pretend to zip up coat
Consonant Digraphs				
/th/	th	*(not voiced)* *(voiced)* **th**umb, **th**in / **th**is, wea**th**er	thumb	make the "thumbs-up" sign
/ng/	ng	ki**ng**, runni**ng**	ring	flap arms as wings

/sh/	sh, ss, ch, ti, ci	**sh**op, mi**ss**ion, **ch**ef, lo**ti**on, spe**ci**al	shark	hold finger to lips (saying "shhhh")
/ch/	ch, tch	**ch**ick, ca**tch**	chick	pretend to tug twice (choo-choo train)
/zh/	s	trea**s**ure, divi**s**ion	treasure chest	pretend to open a treasure chest
/wh/	wh	**wh**ale, **wh**at	whale	shrug shoulders as if saying "what?"
Short Vowel Sounds				
/a/	a	**a**t, **a**pple, r**a**t	apple	pretend to bite an apple
/e/	e, ea	**e**gg, p**e**t, br**ea**d	egg	pretend to crack an egg
/i/	i	**i**f, **i**gloo, s**i**t	igloo	pretend to eat something "icky"
/o/	o	**o**ctopus, h**o**t, s**o**ft	octopus	pretend at doctor's office (say "aaaaah")
/u/	u, o	**u**p, th**u**mb, l**o**ve	umbrella	point up
Long Vowel Sounds				
/A/	a, a_e, ay, ai, ey, ei	t**a**ble, c**a**ke, d**ay**, r**ai**n, th**ey**, **ei**ght	ape	move arms like an ape
/E/	e, e_e, ea, ee, ie, y	m**e**, th**e**se, l**ea**f, b**ee**t, ch**ie**f, bab**y**	eagle	pretend to scream ("eeek")
/I/	i, i_e, igh, y, ie	**I**, f**i**nd, r**i**de, h**igh**, cr**y**, t**ie**	ice	point to self ("I")
/O/	o, o_e, oa, ow	**o**h, b**o**ne, c**oa**t, b**ow**	open	open mouth to form a round "O"
/U/	u, u_e, ew	**u**se, h**u**man, m**u**le, ch**ew**	unicycle	point to another person ("you")
Vowel Diphthongs			**picture with medial or final sound**	
/oo/	oo, u	b**oo**k, p**u**t	book	pretend to read a book
/OO/	oo, u, u_e	t**oo**l, ball**oo**n, r**u**le	moon	pretend to be a ghost, push hands out "oooo"
/ow/	ow, ou, ou_e	c**ow**, **ou**t, m**ou**se	cow	pretend to have a hurt knee ("ouch!")
/oy/	oi, oy	j**oi**n, b**oy**	boy	pretend to oil a door hinge
R-Controled Vowels				
/a(r)/	ar	st**ar**, b**ar**n	car	pretend to drive car
/A(r)/	air, ear, are	h**air**, b**ear**, c**are**	bear	pretend to brush hair
/i(r)/	irr, ere, eer, ear	m**irr**or, h**ere**, d**eer**, h**ear**	deer	cup ear with hand
/o(r)/	or, ore, oor	f**or**, w**ore**, d**oor**	door	pretend to knock on a door
/u(r)/	ur, ir, er, ear, or	t**ur**n, b**ir**d, f**er**n, l**ear**n, w**or**k	bird	pretend to turn a crank

Identifying and Categorizing Phonemes

After children have learned how to isolate initial and final phonemes in words, they will then be ready to identify other words that either begin or end with the same sounds. The following activities will focus on matching sounds word to word. A great resource of words that begin with the same letter is the collection of ABC books on your bookshelf.

Ideas to Introduce Phoneme Identification

Ask your students to sit in a circle. Have a set of real objects or picture cards whose names share the same phoneme in the beginning or ending position. Say the name of each object slowly, emphasizing the targeted sound. Ask two children to each choose an object or picture. Have both children say the names of their selected objects. Then, ask if the sounds at the beginning (or ending) are the same. Have students say the matching sound. Repeat until everyone has had a turn to choose an object.

I Spy Things for Sounds

For a fun and easy way to introduce the concept of matching initial phonemes, collect various common materials whose names begin with the same sound. Begin by locating two or three objects for each sound: /d/, /f/, /l/, /m/, and /t/. Place the collected materials in the center of the playing area. Be sure to add a few objects to the collection that do not fit the criteria. Have children sit in a circle around the objects. Say, "I spy something that starts with the sound /m/." Children can point and take turns naming the objects (e.g, monkey, mouse, marbles, magnets). Continue the game as time and interest allow. Other groups of objects can be collected for these sounds: /h/, /k/, /n/, /p/, /s/, /b/, hard /g/, /v/, /y/, and /z/.

Let's Tell a Story!

Play the I Spy game again as directed above. At the end of each round, choose children to hold the named objects. Continue until everyone has been given an object. Then, invite the children to work in teams and make up an alliterative story (two or three sentences in length) about those objects. As children create their stories, remind them to include any other words they can think of that start with the assigned sound. Encourage them to look at ABC picture books for fun and even silly ideas. When the project is finished, have students tell their stories and act them out for the rest of the class.

Whose Name Begins with . . . ?

Here is another twist on the I Spy game. This time, ask questions that relate to the names of children in your classroom. If more than one child's name starts with the same sound, say, "I am thinking about someone whose name begins with (make the sound). Who is this person?" Children may have to offer more than one answer before guessing the correct name. Alternatively, drop the initial phoneme and then say the name of the child. Invite the class to tell whose name you meant to say. For example, say, "I spy someone in the room whose name ends like _ayla. Who is this person?" (Kayla)

Sorting Sounds—Pages 29–33

Reproduce the Sorting Sounds Cards found on pages 29–33 and the Sorting Board found on page 34. Children can sort the cards according to initial phonemes /b/, /d/, /f/, /g/, /h/, /j/, /k/, /l/, /m/, /n/, /p/, /r/, /s/, /t/, /v/, /w/, /z/ and digraphs /ch/, /sh/, /th/. Have children place the matching cards in one section of the Sorting Board.

Odd One Out!

Select words that either begin or end with the same phoneme. Say the words to a small group of children. Have them simply listen carefully to the words the first time. Ask, "Which word has a different beginning (or ending) sound?" Repeat the words. When they hear the word that doesn't belong, have children make the signal for "out" by raising their hands and pointing with their thumbs just like a baseball umpire.

Where Is the Sound?

To help children visualize the placement of specific sounds in words, work with wooden blocks. Use the block labeled *B* or 1 to represent the beginning sound. Use the block labeled *M* or 2 to represent the middle sound, and use the *E* or 3 block for the ending sound. For example, ask a child, "Where is the /d/ in *dog*?" The child would then pick up the block labeled *B* or 1. Ask, "Where is the /g/ in *dog*?" The child would then pick up the block labeled *E* or 3.

1.
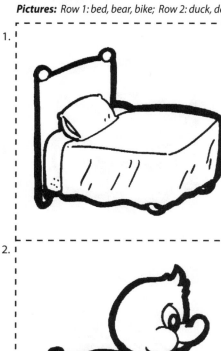

2.

3.

4.

Pictures: *Row 5: hammer, hair, hose; Row 6: jacks, jump, jay; Row 7: kite, kangaroo, king; Row 8: ladder, leaf, lips*

(Identifying and
Categorizing Phonemes)

Pictures: Row 9: mice, marbles, mask; Row 10: nose, nest, nail; Row 11: pear, pie, puppet; Row 12: rose, rattle, ring

(Identifying and Categorizing Phonemes)

Pictures: *Row 13: seal, sail, seeds; Row 14: tail, top, tape; Row 15: van, valentine, violin; Row 16: web, wagon, watch*

(Identifying and Categorizing Phonemes)

13.

14.

15.

16.

Pictures: *Row 17: zipper, zebra, zero; Row 18: chick, chest, cherries; Row 19: shark, sheep, shoes; Row 20: thread, think, thirty-three*

(Identifying and Categorizing Phonemes)

Sorting Board

Blending Phonemes

After children have learned to identify and isolate initial and final consonant sounds, challenge their thought processes by saying words in a segmented manner. For example, if you say /k/-/u/-/b/, have children repeat the sounds quickly until they can hear the word *cub*. Tailor the lessons by first determining how many phonemes the children will blend. For those children in kindergarten, select words that have either two or three phonemes. (See the two- and three-phoneme word lists on pages 24 and 38.) Older students may handle words with up to four phonemes if blends and digraphs have been introduced.

Blending Sounds with Busy Buzzy Bee—Page 37

Busy Buzzy Bee likes to help children learn how to blend sounds. Copy the picture of the bee on page 37 onto colorful card stock and cut it out. Make a Busy Buzzy Bee stick puppet by taping a craft stick to the back of the bee cutout.

Work with a small group of students. Select two or three pictures and arrange them on a flat surface in front of the children. For example, say, "Busy Buzzy Bee wants one of these pictures. Listen carefully to what I say: /c/-/a/-/p/. Which picture does Busy Buzzy Bee want?" Children should then choose the picture of a cap. Repeat the activity with other picture cards as time and interest allow.

Blending Blocks

This activity helps students learn how to see, feel, and hear the sounds in a word. Demonstrate the following steps before children try to blend the sounds. First, show children two blocks of different colors. Explain that each block represents a sound. Touch one block as you say /m/. Then, touch another block and say /E/. (Remember to always demonstrate from left to right as if you are "reading" the sounds.) Finally, touch and move the first block, stretching out the sound /mmmm/ as you slide it toward the second block. Then, when the first block touches the second block, say /EEEE/. The children can hear, feel, and see that the word is *me*.

Begin with words with two phonemes and work up to words with three or more individual sounds.

Say It Slowly, Say It Fast!—Page 37

This fun activity can help children learn how to blend phonemes. Copy the turtle and the rabbit puppet patterns found on page 37. The children can color, cut out, and create puppets by taping them onto craft sticks.

Fill a box or bag with small toys or classroom objects. Pick an object out of the bag and say its name just like the turtle would—very slowly. Then, have the children repeat the word back to you just like the rabbit would—very fast. Repeat in reverse by saying the word quickly and having the children respond slowly.

Finally, when children thoroughly understand the unique workings of phonemes, they will understand that the sequencing and then blending of spoken phonemes creates words. It will become clear, for example, that the phonemes /p/, /e/, and /n/ in that order are the parts of the spoken word *pen*.

Surprise Bag

Fill a bag with classroom objects. Pick an object out of the bag and say its name slowly so that each phoneme is heard. Choose a child to repeat the name, blending the sounds to make the word. That child is next to pick an object from the bag. Again, say the object's name, emphasizing individual sounds. The child chooses a friend to blend the phonemes. Continue until all of the objects have been named.

Guess What?

Choose a food that has a one-syllable name, for example, cake, ham, peach, pie, rice, soup, squash, tea, and so on. Say, "I am thinking of something. It is something you can eat. Guess what it is?" Then, state the name of a food, separating each phoneme. Invite children to respond quickly with the correct food word.

Blending Onsets and Rimes

Use the concept of onset and rimes. Give the children an onset, such as /g/, and the rime /-oat/. Have children put the two together and say "goat."

Here are some of the most common rimes: -ack, -ag, -ail, -ain, -ake, -am, -an, -ang, -ank, -ap, -at, -ay, -ed, -eed, -ell, -en, -est, -ew, -ick, -ight, -ill, -im, -in, -ine, -ing, -ink, -ip, -ob, -ock, -op, -ot, -out, -ore, -ow, -uck, -ug, -um, -un.

Real Sliding

Take learning outside to your school's playground. Provide children with onsets and rimes before they go down the slide. At the top of the slide, the child should say the onset and then the rime separately. When the child reaches the bottom of the slide, he quickly says the whole word.

cat

Help the Robot Talk

Copy the robot puppet pattern below. Color, cut out, and tape the robot onto the front of a small, clean milk carton. Create a pile of small pictures representing words with two and three phonemes. Let children take turns choosing a picture from the pile. Say the name of the object slowly, for example, "You chose a /h/-/a/-/t/." The child should repeat the sentence in a robot voice, blending the phonemes together, "I chose a *hat.*"

Objects in the Room

Say the sounds for the name of an object in the classroom, such as /c/-/l/-/o/-/k/. Stretch the sounds so that students must do the auditory processing to blend the sounds together. Then, ask students to identify the object—*clock.*

As students become more comfortable with blending sounds, let them move plastic alphabet letters as they hear the sounds. Begin by sounding out simple CVC words or CCVC words to help them begin to connect sounds with graphemes. Slowly say the sounds of a word. Students should move the letters that correspond to the sounds.

Robot Puppet Pattern

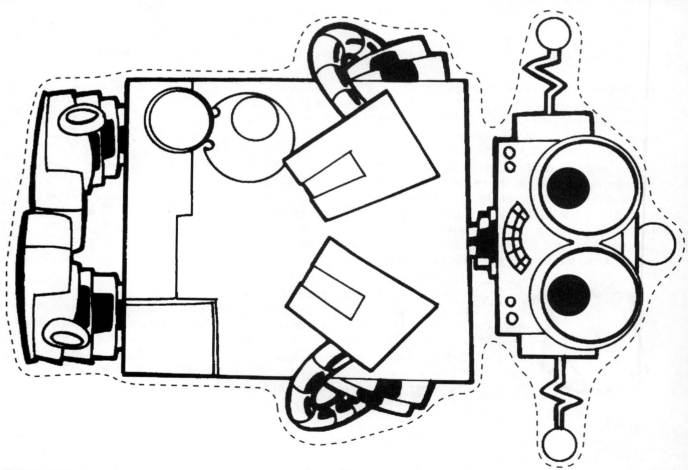

Rabbit, Turtle, and Bee Patterns

(Directions are found on page 35.)

Teaching Tips for Kids with Dyslexia

Segmenting Phonemes

When children can demonstrate the skill of blending isolated phonemes to create words, have them do the reverse skill: listening to whole words and then separating the sounds in those words. *Phoneme segmentation* is asking the student to separate a word into its speech sounds (phonemes). For example, remind students that every word is made up of sounds. Then say, "Listen to this word, *dog*—/d/- /o/-/g/. Let's count the sounds in the word *dog*—/d/-/o/-/g/." Have students use their fingers or move a block for each sound they hear in the word.

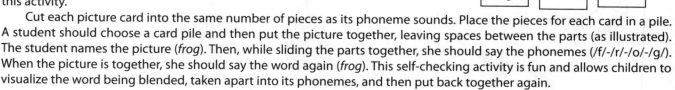

Segmenting and Blending Picture/Puzzle Cards—Page 40

This is a wonderful activity for children to visually see how words can be blended together and then segmented or taken apart. Copy, color, cut out, and laminate the cards provided on page 40 or use any picture cards of your choice for this activity.

Cut each picture card into the same number of pieces as its phoneme sounds. Place the pieces for each card in a pile. A student should choose a card pile and then put the picture together, leaving spaces between the parts (as illustrated). The student names the picture (*frog*). Then, while sliding the parts together, she should say the phonemes (/f/-/r/-/o/-/g/). When the picture is together, she should say the word again (*frog*). This self-checking activity is fun and allows children to visualize the word being blended, taken apart into its phonemes, and then put back together again.

I Spy Segmenting and Blending

Play a variation of I Spy to develop your students' skills in segmenting and blending phonemes. Begin by saying to the class, "I spy something in our room. Listen carefully to its name because I'm going to say its name a silly way. I spy a /f/-/i/-/sh/. Can you guess what it is?"

After children have practiced blending sounds, vary the I Spy game by inviting children to choose and segment words for you to blend. Begin by using words with only two or three individual sounds and work up to words with four or more sounds, such as /b/-/r/-/i/-/k/ (*brick*).

Following are examples of words for students to segment and blend.

ape	book	broom	desk	fish	moose	phone	soap	truck
ball	bow	cap	dog	glass	pan	shoe	stool	wig
barn	bread	cat	dress	ice	pea	skate	tie	zoo
bean	brick	cheese	eel	jump	pen	slip	train	

Working in Pairs—Page 41

Have students work with partners. Each partner team will need a set of game cards found on page 41. As a whole class, say the name of each picture, segment the word into its individual phonemes, and finally count how many phonemes are in the word. Have one of the partners write the correct number of phonemes on the back of each of the game cards.

Now, the children can work as teams. They should pick up a card, together say the word, segment the word into phonemes, count the phonemes, and then self-check their answers by looking on the back of the card. Have the partners place all of the cards they segmented correctly in one pile and cards that need additional practice in another pile. Children love to be able to check their own responses. It also helps build self-confidence when they can see how often their answers were correct. You will also find it valuable to check your students' card piles to see which words need additional practice. You may see a pattern in the phonemes that students are not hearing or processing accurately.

Phonemes in Our Names

Collect a photograph of each child, tape the photos on sheets of paper, and then photocopy them to create picture cards. Follow the directions for the Working in Pairs activity (above), but make game cards using the children's photos and names. This variation may require a higher level of skill as students count the phonemes in the multisyllable names of their classmates.

Banking on Sounds

Each student will need a copy of the Banking on Sounds piggy bank pattern on page 39 and at least 10 pennies. Generate words from classroom materials or from a favorite children's book. As you say a word, children should place a penny in the piggy bank for each phoneme they hear.

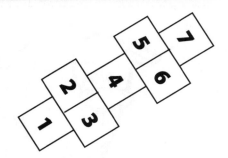

Phoneme Count Hopscotch

Create a traditional hopscotch pattern, either with chalk outdoors or with masking tape in your classroom (see illustration). Say a word and then have a child count out the phonemes as he hops on the hopscotch squares. For example, if the word is *cow*, the student would say /k/ and hop on the number 1 and then say /ow/ and hop on the number 2. The last number reinforces the total number of phonemes heard in the word. Children who have a difficult time sitting still will love this activity!

Phoneme Beanbag Toss

Draw a four-square grid with chalk outside or use masking tape inside. Write 1, 2, 3, or 4 in each square. Have a pile of picture cards ready for the children. The first child tosses the beanbag onto one of the numerals. For example, if the child's beanbag lands on 3, the child should look through the pictures and find one whose name has three phonemes. This activity is much more difficult than simply being asked to segment a particular word. The children must analyze several cards before choosing one that matches the same number of phonemes as the number on which the beanbag landed.

Banking on Sounds Piggy Bank Pattern

(Directions are found on page 38.)

card 1

card 5

card 2

card 6

card 3

card 7

card 4

card 8

Answer key: 1./k/ /ow/   2./b/ /E/   3./b/ /O/ /t/   4./sh/ /a(r)/ /k/   5./f/ /i/ /sh/   6./b/ /l/ /o/ /k/   7./f/ /r/ /o/ /g/   8./t/ /i/ /g/ /u(r)/

Pictures: *Row 1: dog, fish, tub, car; Row 2: jar, box, book, drum;*
Row 3: rope, cheese, chair, peach; Row 4: pig, coat, key, kite; Row 5: cow, star, jet, slide

1.

2.

3.

4.

5.

Manipulating Phonemes

The most difficult skills when changing individual sounds in spoken words are to substitute, delete, and add phonemes to build new words. Only after children have had rich experiences working with rhyming words, recognizing alliterative phrases, isolating sounds, and blending and segmenting phonemes would it be appropriate for them to manipulate phonemes in word-play games and lessons. The following examples explain further how to use these advanced phonemic awareness skills:

❑ **Phoneme Substitution: when one phoneme is substituted for another phoneme. For example, begin with the word *bug*. Change /b/ to /m/, and the word *bug* is changed to *mug*; or change /g/ to /n/, and the word *bug* is changed to *bun*.**

To practice this skill, first have children answer word riddles using initial consonants as onsets with rimes. Then, proceed to riddles that incorporate initial blends and digraphs as onsets. (See The Best Word Families and Rhyming Words for Beginners on page 17 for onset and rime ideas.) For example: What word begins with /m/ and rhymes with *top*? (*mop*) What word begins with /dr/ and rhymes with *top*? (*drop*) What word begins with /ch/ and rhymes with *top*? (*chop*)

❑ **Phoneme Deletion: when one phoneme is removed, leaving a different, recognizable word. For example, the word *block* without /b/ is *lock*; or the word *cart* without /t/ is *car*.**

When children can easily hear and count individual phonemes in words, then they are ready to try deleting sounds to make new words. For example: Take away the /f/ sound in the word *flock*. What is the new word? (*lock*) Take away the /t/ sound in the word *train*. What is the new word? (*rain*) The answers do not always have to be actual words. For additional practice, have children answer riddles like these: What "word" would be left if you take away the /k/ sound in *snack*? (*sna*) If you take away the /s/ sound in *snack*? (*nack*) For another example: What word do you have if you take away the /p/ sound in *clamp*? (*clam*) If you take away the /k/ sound in *clamp*? (*lamp*) If you take away the /l/ sound in *clamp*? (*camp*)

❑ **Phoneme Addition: when a new word is made by adding a phoneme to the original word. For example, add /s/ to the beginning of *tar* to change the word to *star*; or add /t/ to the end of *tar* to change the word to *tart*.**

To strengthen this skill, generate riddles that ask children to add certain sounds to chosen phonograms or words. This type of exercise is also an effective way to introduce a read-aloud book that incorporates wonderful language play in its title. Check your bookshelf for potential activity ideas. For example, before reading aloud the book *Smash! Mash! Crash! There Goes the Trash!* by Barbara Odanaka, think of word riddles for the -ash family. Examples include the following: What word rhymes with *ash* and begins with /b/? (*bash*) Begins with /d/? (*dash*) Begins with /l/? (*lash*) What word do you have if you add /f/ to *lash*? (*flash*) If you add /s/? (*slash*) If you add /k/? (*clash*) What word do you have if you add /s/ to *mash*? (*smash*) If you add /t/ to *rash*? (*trash*) If you add /k/? (*crash*) After this fun word play activity, everyone will be ready to read more about trash!

Play Add-On and Take Away

Give children words and ask them to repeat the word minus a sound or with an additional sound. For example: Take away the /k/ from *monkey*. (*money*) Add /l/ to *feet* to make what word? (*fleet*)

Sample Read-Aloud Books

No doubt, there are wonderful picture books with delightful language play already on your bookshelf. Try to locate titles with lively story lines, rhyming patterns, or strings of nonsense words that draw attention to sounds. To locate good children's literature, see Children's Books and Songs to Increase Phonemic Awareness found on pages 45 and 46. Here are some additional selections which are perfect for practicing the manipulation of phonemes.

❑ *The Cow That Went OINK* by Bernard Most (Harcourt Brace Jovanovich, 1990)

❑ *Rub-a-Dub Sub* by Linda Ashman (Harcourt Brace Jovanovich, 2003)

❑ *Rattletrap Car* by Phyllis Root (Candlewick Press, 2001)

❑ Dr. Seuss titles—choose your favorites!

Sing Songs

Sing familiar songs and change the phonemes in the chorus. For example, change the *ee-i-ee-i-o* in "Old MacDonald" to *mee-i-mee-i-toe* or change the chorus in "The Farmer in the Dell" from *hi-ho-the-dario, the farmer in the dell* to *di-do-the-mario, the charmer in the well*. Children will giggle as they think of funny new choruses for the songs they know. Continue to help children gain experience with recognizing that when a phoneme is removed, added, or substituted, a new word is created. Use the examples below to get started.

Phoneme Manipulation Examples

Here are some words to use when practicing with students:

Deletion of Beginning Phonemes

the word: *blast*—take away /b/ = *last*
the word: *bread*—take away /b/ = *read*
the word: *candy*—take away /k/ = *Andy*
the word: *cow*—take away /c/ = *ow*
the word: *deer*—take away /d/ = *ear*
the word: *farm*—take away /f/ = *arm*
the word: *feet*—take away /f/ = *eat*
the word: *gate*—take away /g/ = *ate*
the word: *leg*—take away /l/ = *egg*
the word: *seal*—take away /s/ = *eel*
the word: *skid*—take away /s/ = *kid*
the word: *smile*—take away /s/ = *mile*
the word: *tape*—take away /t/ = *ape*
the word: *tie*—take away /t/ = *I or eye*
the word: *towel*—take away /t/ = *owl*

Deletion of Final Phonemes

the word: *bean*—take away /n/ = *bee*
the word: *boat*—take away /t/ = *bow*
the word: *boil*—take away /l/ = *boy*
the word: *bowl*—take away /l/ = *bow*
the word: *cart*—take away /t/ = *car*
the word: *dollar*—take away /a(r)/ = *doll*
the word: *ice*—take away /s/ = *I or eye*
the word: *pillow*—take away /O/ = *pill*
the word: *pipe*—take away /p/ = *pie*
the word: *shelf*—take away /f/ = *shell*
the word: *team*—take away /m/ = *tea*

Adding Beginning Phonemes

the word: *ear*—add /t/ = *tear*
the word: *ice*—add /r/ = *rice*
the word: *it*—add /s/ = *sit*
the word: *lake*—add /f/ = *flake*
the word: *lap*—add /c/ = *clap*
the word: *last*—add /b/ = *blast*
the word: *lid*—add /s/ = *slid*
the word: *lock*—add /c/ = *clock*
the word: *nail*—add /s/ = *snail*
the word: *pace*—add /s/ = *space*
the word: *rain*—add /t/ = *train*
the word: *top*—add /s/ = *stop*

Substitution of Beginning Phonemes

the word: *bike*—change /b/ to /l/ = *like*
the word: *bone*—change /b/ to /f/ = *phone*
the word: *cake*—change /k/ to /r/ = *rake*
the word: *cat*—change /k/ to /r/ = *rat*
the word: *cot*—change /k/ to /d/ = *dot*
the word: *dice*—change /d/ to /m/ = *mice*
the word: *dog*—change /d/ to /f/ = *fog*
the word: *fan*—change /f/ to /k/ = *can*
the word: *goat*—change /g/ to /b/ = *boat*
the word: *hen*—change /h/ to /p/ = *pen*
the word: *hose*—change /h/ to /r/ = *rose*
the word: *house*—change /h/ to /m/ = *mouse*
the word: *ring*—change /r/ to /w/ = *wing*
the word: *ten*—change /t/ to /h/ = *hen*

Substitution of Final Phonemes

the word: *bun*—change /n/ to /t/ = *but*
the word: *bus*—change /s/ to /g/ = *bug*
the word: *can*—change /n/ to /t/ = *cat*
the word: *cow*—change /ow/ to /E/ = *key*
the word: *doll*—change /l/ to /k/ = *dock*
the word: *fat*—change /t/ to /n/ = *fan*
the word: *fin*—change /n/ to /sh/ = *fish*
the word: *five*—change /v/ to /l/ = *file*
the word: *game*—change /m/ to /t/ = *gate*
the word: *kiss*—change /s/ to /ng/ = *king*
the word: *pig*—change /g/ to /n/ = *pin*
the word: *rail*—change /l/ to /n/ = *rain*
the word: *sent*—change /t/ to /d/ = *send*
the word: *wish*—change /sh/ to /ng/ = *wing*

Substitution of Medial Phonemes

the word: *bat*—change /a/ to /e/ = *bet*
the word: *bell*—change /e/ to /i/ = *bill*
the word: *bike*—change /I/ to /A/ = *bake*
the word: *boot*—change /OO/ to /a/ = *bat*
the word: *cat*—change /a/ to /i/ = *kit*
the word: *cub*—change /u/ to /a/ = *cab*
the word: *mile*—change /I/ to /U/ = *mule*
the word: *moon*—change /OO/ to /a/ = *man*
the word: *pail*—change /A/ to /OO/ = *pool*
the word: *phone*—change /O/ to /i/ = *fin*
the word: *pin*—change /i/ to /e/ = *pen*

Substituting Phonemes–
Three Different Activities

Name:

Teacher Directions:
Cut off , choose an activity, and orally give instructions to students. Have them circle each picture that shows the new word.

Substituting Beginning Phonemes:

1. *cat* change /c/ to /b/ = *bat*
2. *dog* change /d/ to /l/ = *log*
3. *pail* change /p/ to /n/ = *nail*
4. *cub* change /c/ to /t/ = *tub*
5. *pen* change /p/ to/h/ = *hen*
6. *bug* change /b/ to /r/ = *rug*
7. *pig* change /p/ to /w/ = *wig*
8. *boat* change /b/ to /g/ = *goat*

Substituting Final Phonemes:

1. *cat* change /t/ to /n/ =*can*
2. *dog* change /g/ to /l/ = *doll*
3. *pail* change /l/ to /n/ = *pain*
4. *cub* change /b/ to /t/ = *cut*
5. *pen* change /n/ to/t/ = *pet*
6. *bug* change /g/ to /s/ = *bus*
7. *pig* change /g/ to /n/ = *pin*
8. *boat* change /t/ to /n/ = *bone*

Substituting Medial Phonemes:

1. *cat* change /a/ to /u/ = *cut*
2. *dog* change /o/ to /i/ = *dig*
3. *pail* change /A/ to /OO/ = *pool*
4. *cub* change /u/ to /a/ = *cab*
5. *pen* change /e/ to/a/ = *pan*
6. *bug* change /u/ to /a/ = *bag*
7. *pig* change /i/ to /e/ = *peg*
8. *boat* change /O/ to /a/ = *bat*

Children's Books and Songs to Increase Phonemic Awareness

Books

- [ ] *ABC I Like Me.* Nancy Carlson. (Viking, 1997)
- [ ] *Altoona Baboona.* Janie Bynum. (Harcourt, 1999)
- [ ] *Amelia Bedelia.* Peggy Parish. (HarperTrophy, 1992)
- [ ] *Asana and the Animals: A Book of Pet Poems.* Grace Nichols. (Candlewick Press, 1997)
- [ ] *Bear Snores On.* Karma Wilson. (Margaret K. McElderry, 2002)
- [ ] *The Best Storybook Ever.* Richard Scarry. (Golden Books, 2000)
- [ ] *The Biggest Tongue Twister Book in the World.* Gyles Daubeney Brandreth. (Sterling Publishing, 1981)
- [ ] *Blue Bowl Down: An Applalachian Rhyme.* C. M. Millen. (Candlewick Press, 2004)
- [ ] *Bowl Patrol.* Marilyn Janovitz. (North South Books, 1996)
- [ ] *Bubble Gum, Bubble Gum.* Lisa Wheeler. (Megan Tingley, 2004)
- [ ] *Bus Stop, Bus Go!* Daniel Kirk. (Putnam, 2001)
- [ ] *Casey Jones.* Allan Drummond. (Farrar, Straus, and Giroux, 2001)
- [ ] *The Cat Barked.* Lydia Monks. (Dial Books, 1999)
- [ ] *Cat in the Hat.* Dr. Seuss. (Random House, 1957)
- [ ] *Chugga-Chugga Choo-Choo.* Kevin Lewis. (Hyperion, 1999)
- [ ] *Clara Ann Cookie, Go to Bed!* Harriet Ziefert. (Walter Lorraine Books, 2000)
- [ ] *Clever Crow.* Cynthia DeFelice. (Atheneum, 1998)
- [ ] *Dinosaur Chase.* Carolyn Otto. (HarperCollins, 1991)
- [ ] *Dinosaur Roar!* Paul Stickland, Henrietta Stickland. (Dutton Books, 1997)
- [ ] *A Dragon in a Wagon.* Lynley Dodd. (Gareth Stevens Publishing, 2000)
- [ ] *Dumpy LaRue.* Elizabeth Winthrop. (Henry Holt and Co., 2004)
- [ ] *Edwina the Emu.* Sheena Knowles. (HarperTrophy, 1997)
- [ ] *Faint Frogs Feeling Feverish: And Other Terrifically Tantalizing Tongue Twisters.* Lilian Obligado. (Puffin Books, 1996)
- [ ] *"Fire! Fire!" Said Mrs. McGuire.* Bill Martin Jr. (Voyager Books, 1999)
- [ ] *Fox in Socks.* Dr. Seuss. (Random House, 1965)
- [ ] *Frog Went a-Courtin'.* John Langstaff. (Gulliver Books, 1955)
- [ ] *A Giraffe and a Half.* Shel Silverstein. (HarperCollins, 1964)
- [ ] *Good Night Pillow Fight.* Sally Cook. (Joanna Cotler, 2004)
- [ ] *Grandma's Cat.* Helen Ketteman. (Houghton Mifflin, 1996)
- [ ] *Green Eggs and Ham.* Dr. Seuss. (Random House, 1960)
- [ ] *Greetings, Sun.* Phillis Gershator and David Gershator. (Dorling Kindersley, 1998)
- [ ] *The Happy Day.* Ruth Krauss. (HarperCollins, 1949)
- [ ] *The Helen Oxenbury Nursery Story Book.* Helen Oxenbury. (Knopf Books, 1985)
- [ ] *Henny Penny.* Paul Galdone. (Clarion Books, 1979)
- [ ] *The Hokey Pokey.* Larry La Prise. (Simon & Schuster, 1996)
- [ ] *Honk! Toot! Beep!* Samantha Berger. (Cartwheel Books, 2001)
- [ ] *A House Is a House for Me.* Mary Ann Hoberman. (Viking, 1978)
- [ ] *How Big Is a Pig?* Clare Beaton. (Turtleback Books Distributed, 2003)
- [ ] *I Can Fly.* Ruth Krauss. (Simon & Schuster, 1955)
- [ ] *I Love Trains!* Philemon Sturges. (HarperCollins, 2001)
- [ ] *I Love You, Good Night.* Jon Buller. (Simon & Schuster, 1988)
- [ ] *Inch by Inch: The Garden Song.* David Mallett. (HarperTrophy, 1995)
- [ ] *I Saw the Sea and the Sea Saw Me.* Megan Montague Cash. (Viking, 2001)
- [ ] *Is Your Mama a Llama?* Deborah Guarino. (Scholastic, 1997)
- [ ] *Jesse Bear, What Will You Wear?* Nancy White Carlstrom. (Simon & Schuster, 1986)
- [ ] *Llama Llama Red Pajama.* Anna Dewdney. (Viking, 2005)
- [ ] *Louelle Mae, She's Run Away!* Karen Beaumont Alarcon. (Henry Holt and Co., 1997)
- [ ] *Madeline.* Ludwig Bemelmans. (Viking, 1958)
- [ ] *Messy Bessy.* Pat McKissack and Frederick McKissack. (Children's Press, 1987)
- [ ] *Mice Twice.* Joseph Low. (Aladdin, 1986)
- [ ] *Miss Spider Series.* David Kirk. (Scholastic, 2000)
- [ ] *Mole in a Hole.* Rita Golden Gelman. (Random House, 2000)
- [ ] *Mother Goose: A Collection of Classic Nursery Rhymes.* Michael Hague. (Henry Holt, 1984)
- [ ] *Mrs. Brown Went to Town.* Wong Herbert Yee. (Houghton Mifflin, 1996)

- ❑ *Mrs. McTats and Her Houseful of Cats.* Alyssa Satin Capucilli. (Margaret K. McElderry, 2001)
- ❑ *Mrs. Nosh and the Great Big Squash.* Sarah Weeks. (Scholastic, 2001)
- ❑ *Mrs. Wishy Washy.* Joy Cowley. (Philomel, 1999)
- ❑ *My Crayons Talk.* Patricia Hubbard. (Henry Holt and Co., 1996)
- ❑ *My Grandma Lived in Gooligulch.* Graeme Base. (Harry N. Abrams, 1990)
- ❑ *My Very First Mother Goose.* Iona Archibald Opie. (Candlewick Press, 1996)
- ❑ *Nana's Hog.* Larry Dane Brimner. (Children's Press, 1999)
- ❑ *Nathaniel Willy, Scared Silly.* Judith Mathews. (Bradbury Press, 1994)
- ❑ *Nora's Room.* Jessica Harper. (HarperCollins, 2001)
- ❑ *Pass the Peas, Please.* Dina Anastasio. (Warner Books, 1990)
- ❑ *Pat-a-Cake and Other Play Rhymes.* Joanna Cole and Stephanie Calmenson. (Morrow, 1992)
- ❑ *Pickles in My Soup.* Mary Pearson. (Children's Press, 2000)
- ❑ *A Pinky Is a Baby Mouse and Other Baby Animal Names.* Pam Munoz Ryan. (Hyperion, 1997)
- ❑ *A Place to Bloom.* Lorianne Siomades. (Boyds Mills Press, 1997)
- ❑ *Play Rhymes.* Marc Tolon Brown. (Puffin Books, 1993)
- ❑ *Poems to Read to the Very Young.* Josette Frank. (Random House, 1988)
- ❑ *The Random House Book of Poetry for Children.* Jack Prelutsky. (Random House, 1983)
- ❑ *Read-Aloud Rhymes for the Very Young.* Jack Prelutsky. (Knopf Books, 1986)
- ❑ *Rub a Dub Dub.* Kin Eagle. (Charlesbridge Publishing, 1999)
- ❑ *Scat, Cats.* Joan Holub. (Puffin Books, 2001)
- ❑ *Shhhhh! Everybody's Sleeping.* Julie Markes. (HarperCollins, 2005)
- ❑ *Sing a Song of Popcorn.* Beatrice Schenk de Regniers. (Scholastic, 1988)
- ❑ *Six Sleepy Sheep.* Jeffie Ross Gordon. (Boyds Mills Press, 1991)
- ❑ *Skunks.* David T. Greenberg. (Megan Tingley, 2001)
- ❑ *Slinky Malinki.* Lynley Dodd. (Tricycle Press, 2005)
- ❑ *Some Smug Slug.* Pamela Duncan Edwards. (HarperCollins, 1996)
- ❑ *Splat.* Mary Margaret Perez-Mercado. (Children's Press, 2000)
- ❑ *Stop That Noise!* Paul Geraghty. (Knopf, 1993)
- ❑ *Surprises Collection.* Lee Bennett Hopkins. (Harper & Row, 1984)
- ❑ *10 in the Bed.* Anne Geddes. (Andrews McMeel Publishing, 2001)
- ❑ *There Was an Old Witch.* Howard Reeves. (Hyperion, 2000)
- ❑ *There's a Wocket in My Pocket.* Dr. Seuss. (Random House, 1974)
- ❑ *The Three Wishes.* Judith Bauer Stamper. (Cartwheel Books, 1998)
- ❑ *Time of Wonder.* Robert McCloskey. (Viking Books, 1957)
- ❑ *Tiny Tim Collection.* Jill Bennett. (Delacorte Press, 1982)
- ❑ *Tomie de Paola's Mother Goose.* Tomie dePaola. (Putnam, 1985)
- ❑ *Top Cat.* Lois Ehlert. (Harcourt, 1998)
- ❑ *Truck Talk: Rhyme on Wheels.* Bobbi Katz. (Cartwheel Books, 1997)
- ❑ *Uno, Dos, Tres = One, Two, Three.* Pat Mora. (Clarion Books, 1996)
- ❑ *Watch William Walk.* Ann Jonas. (Greenwillow, 1997)
- ❑ *When the Dark Comes Dancing: A Bedtime Poetry Book.* Nancy Larrick. (Putnam, 1983)
- ❑ *Where the Sidewalk Ends.* Shel Silverstein. (HarperCollins, 1974)
- ❑ *Where the Wild Things Are.* Maurice Sendak. (HarperCollins, 1988)
- ❑ *Which Witch Is Which?* Judi Barrett. (Atheneum, 2001)
- ❑ *Who Is Tapping at My Window?* A. G. Deming. (Dutton Books, 1988)
- ❑ *Wiggle.* Doreen Cronin. (Atheneum, 2005)

Songs

- ❑ *American Folk, Game & Activity Songs.* Pete Seeger. (Smithsonian Folkways, 2000)
- ❑ *American Folk Songs for Children.* Mike Seeger and Peggy Seeger. (Rounder Select, 1997)
- ❑ *Children's Favorite Songs.* Walt Disney Records. (Disney, 1991)
- ❑ *A Child's Celebration of Song.* Music for Little People. (Music Little People, 1992)
- ❑ *Little White Duck.* Burl Ives. (Sony Wonder, 1991)
- ❑ *Muppet Hits.* The Muppets. (Zoom Express, 1993)
- ❑ *Old Mr. Mackle Hackle.* Gunnar Madsen. (G-Spot, 1999)
- ❑ *Peter, Paul and Mommy.* Peter, Paul, and Mary. (Warner Bros, 1990)
- ❑ *Raffi Singable Songs Collection.* Raffi. (Rounder, 1996)
- ❑ *Really Silly Songs About Animals.* Bethie. (Discovery House Music, 1993)
- ❑ *Songs to Grow On for Mother and Child.* Woody Guthrie. (Smithsonian Folkways, 1992)
- ❑ *You Sing a Song and I'll Sing a Song.* Ella Jenkins. (Smithsonian Folkways, 1992)

Multisensory Systematic Sequential Phonics

Once children have developed an understanding of phonemic awareness they are ready to learn how to read. That sounds like an ominous task—especially for children with dyslexia! Fortunately, there is a wealth of well-documented research from the National Institute of Child Health and Human Development (NICHD) that validates instructional strategies proven to help children with reading disabilities learn how to read.

One of the most effective instructional methods combines using **multisensory teaching strategies** along with a **systematic sequential phonics** approach. This means that the child will be learning through more than one sense—with each lesson incorporating auditory, visual, and kinesthetic experiences. The multisensory teaching strategies are teamed with phonics instruction that is systematic, in that it follows a scope and sequence, and directly teaches and consistently reviews sound-spelling relationships. The combination of these instructional approachs will lead to better reading.

One of the oldest and most widely recognized programs for teaching reading to children with dyslexia is the **Orton-Gillingham Multisensory Method.** This method was developed in the early 1930s by Dr. Samuel Orton and Anna Gillingham and is still used today. Dr. Orton was the first to identify the syndrome of developmental reading disability (dyslexia) and created an effective remedial approach. Anna Gillingham trained teachers in his approach and then compiled these instructional methods with Bessie W. Stillman in the book, *The Orton–Gillingham Manual: Remedial Training for Children with Specific Disability in Reading, Spelling and Penmanship*, published in 1935.

A systematic sequential phonics approach directly and explicitly teaches:

❑ phonemic awareness

❑ phoneme/grapheme correspondence that teaches how to take the individual letters or sounds and put them together to form a word, as well as how to look at a long word and break it into smaller pieces

❑ six types of syllables and how those syllables affect vowel sounds

❑ specific rules that apply to written words, presented one at a time

❑ roots and affixes

❑ sight words with irregular spelling.

> **Each new concept or rule must be specifically taught and then practiced until the child is able to use it effectively in both reading and spelling.**

Unfortunately, most children with dyslexia are identified after they have already experienced reading failure. By the time most of these children get help they feel discouraged and are confused about written language. It is crucial that the teacher go back and reteach reading skills from the very beginning. This will build a strong foundation that is essential for the child's future success. Remember, ALL children must go through the same stages of reading whether they have dyslexia or not. The child with dyslexia will better understand written language by learning one rule at a time, then practicing that rule until it can be used automatically and fluently when reading and spelling.

A multisensory approach involves visual, auditory, and kinesthetic senses:

❑ The child sees (visual) the letter or word

❑ The child says (auditory) the letter sound or says the word

❑ The child writes or traces (kinesthetic) the letter or word—using large muscles (pretending to write in the air) and small muscles (using a fingertip to write in sand or tracing on a screen with words placed under it)

Other important considerations:

❑ Each child's program is individualized—no two programs should look exactly alike.

❑ Instruction for children with dyslexia should be more intense, requiring more practice.

❑ Continuous assessment is crucial so that children make consistent progress.

Chapter Three
Reading, Spelling, and Writing Tips
Multisensory Methods for Teaching Letters and Sight Words

Research conducted by the National Institute of Child Health and Human Development has shown that multisensory teaching methods are by far the most effective strategies for helping children with reading disabilities, including those children with dyslexia, learn how to read. A multisensory approach enables children to learn by utilizing more than one sense.

The following multisensory activities may be used to help children learn alphabet letters as well as learn how to read crucial high-frequency, or sight, words.

Modeling Clay—Learning Letters or Sight Words

Play dough or modeling clay is probably the **best tactile material** children with reading disabilities can use. Clay can be used to model individual letters and to create high-frequency words.

For children who need to have visual images of words, a clay model can serve as that visual representation. For example, provide children with a variety of pictures that represent nouns and the three letters *a*, *n*, and *d* to spell *and* molded in clay. Have a child lay out a picture card (cat), the clay word *and*, and another picture card (dog). The child can then practice reading "cat and dog." Using clay to teach words that do not have a visual picture can significantly increase a child's word recognition skills of sight and high-frequency words.

Beginning readers and struggling readers recognize very few words instantly. Through repeated exposure to the same words, and with multisensory experiences, children can significantly increase the number of words they are able to instantly identify. The 25 most common words (see below) make up approximately one-fourth to one-third of all reading material. Instant recognition of these words can also have an incredible impact on increasing a child's reading speed and comprehension.

The 25 Most Common Words

1. the	4. to	7. of	10. he	13. was	16. his	19. with	22. but	24. one
2. and	5. in	8. it	11. she	14. for	17. her	20. are	23. at	25. said
3. a	6. you	9. is	12. that	15. I	18. they	21. be		

The 100 Most Used Words

List 1		List 2		List 3		List 4	
and	out	are	make	all	let	away	much
boy	play	at	new	am	me	blue	need
can	read	but	now	ask	must	every	old
come	see	could	one	do	my	father	put
did	the	doing	said	down	of	from	ran
girl	this	eat	she	for	over	green	red
go	to	get	they	good	so	had	ride
help	us	going	two	has	some	house	run
like	want	he	use	have	that	how	there
man	will	here	we	him	them	in	walk
mother	with	it	were	is	thing	just	was
not	work	look	would	keep	what	little	went
	you		your		why		yellow

Creating Multisensory Letters and Words

Teach new high-frequency words in isolation first, providing fun activities that center around the individual word. For example, introduce new words and then allow children to mold the words with clay (see page 49). Offer other opportunities for children to "feel" the new words as well. After the children are familiar with the new word, have them start to use the word in context.

Here are some additional ideas for creating multisensory letters and words:

❑ Fill a cookie sheet with sand or rice and then practice printing letters and words.

❑ Bend chenille stems into letters and lay out the letters to form words.

❑ Trace over letters and words on tracing paper or vellum.

❑ Finger paint letters and words. Add glitter or salt to the paint to create an additional texture.

❑ Add various scents, such as mint or lemon extract, to finger paint to add the sense of smell.

❑ Print letters and words on paper plates using edible substances, such as yogurt, peanut butter, and pudding.

❑ Provide an old typewriter or a computer and allow children to type words.

❑ Mix white glue with tempera paint or provide glitter glue for children to use to practice printing letters or write high-frequency words. When the glue is dry, the children can "feel" what they wrote.

❑ Make "telegrams" by cutting words out of newspapers or magazines. Paste the messages on blank paper. Children can read the messages to their friends. It is suggested that you clip words from advertisements because they generally have the largest type.

Enlarged Versions of the Printed Page and Highlighters

Providing children with enlarged versions of the page can be extremely helpful. Children can use highlighters to mark difficult words. You may also highlight new words in the text prior to having children read the selection. This helps remind children of any new words.

My Own Word or Picture Dictionary

Provide each child with a notebook that has an alphabet letter in the upper right-hand corner of every page (one letter per page). As children learn new words, they can add them to the correct pages. Children should write the word, illustrate it if possible, and be encouraged to write the word in a sentence, using it correctly.

As the words begin to fill up the dictionaries, the children's self-confidence will increase. It is rewarding for children to actually "see" that they are learning to read and understand more and more words! Children will also benefit from looking up words in their own dictionaries.

Bingo and Lotto Games

Teacher-made (or commercially purchased) bingo and lotto games are always fun for children to play and are excellent activities for reinforcing high-frequency word recognition. Bingo games help children recognize words auditorily, while lotto games help children to recognize words visually while they are matching them.

Sight Word Hopscotch

You will need a discarded plastic window shade or vinyl tablecloth and a permanent black marker. Draw a hopscotch grid and write a high-frequency word in each section. The children can jump on and say each word as they hop on the grid. Children can also use beanbags to toss onto each word. This activity provides a visual, auditory, and kinesthetic learning experience.

Word Wall Excitement

Many teachers are now using word walls—there is no doubt about their effectiveness for reinforcing words and for motivating young readers. Read all of the words on your word wall every day! Each day, children will become more confident, and their reading speed will increase.

Be creative with the classroom word walls. For example, tape the cards to colorful streamers for a circus theme. Another option would be to place each word on an alphabet letter planet; for example, the "Big *Bb*" planet would display words like *big*, *but*, and *boy*. Or, make an "Around the Town" word wall, having each letter be the name of a building and showing the words in the windows.

Word Chunks

It is an exciting time for children when they realize that not every word needs to be learned as an entirely new word! Many words have "chunks," or phonograms, that are already known. For example, a child that has learned to read the word *at* might realize that the word *at* can easily be turned into the words *cat*, *hat*, and *rat*.

Make banners or posters with word chunks written on the top and add words as the children are able to identify them.

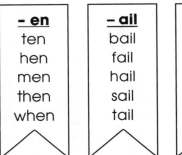

– en	– ail	– oat
ten	bail	boat
hen	fail	coat
men	hail	goat
then	sail	moat
when	tail	float

Word Substitution Games

This activity is extremely useful when introducing a new theme or topic or a new high-frequency word. Write several sentences in which the same key word has been omitted. As the paragraph progresses, each sentence should reveal more clues about the meaning of the key word. Using an overhead projector, show the paragraph one sentence at a time to the children. Record several students' responses as they predict what word goes in the blanks.

> **Example:** The answer to these sentences is *dog.*
> A _____ can be a fun. Everybody would like a _____.
> If you have a _____, you can do many things together.
> You can go to the park with your _____.
> A _____ is someone who likes you.
> A _____ can play fetch with you.
> A _____ can chew bones.

Hide-and-Seek Words

Write the selected words on index cards and then hide the cards all around the room. Children will love to search for the words. As each word card is found, have the child read the word to you.

American Sign Language Can Increase Language and Literacy Skills

Exciting research currently being conducted is focused on documenting the effects that learning sign language has on the development of language and literacy skills of young hearing children. In two different studies (Capirci, 1998), ASL was taught in context to children during their first- and second-grade years. The children in both studies who received the instruction scored higher on tests in visual discrimination and spatial memory than did the groups of children who did not receive any signing instruction. Additional studies (Daniels, 1994) have consistently found that young hearing children of hearing parents who learned ASL in a school context demonstrated a greater understanding of English vocabulary and achieved higher scores on the Peabody Picture Vocabulary Test (PPVT) than their peers who did not receive any instruction.

It has also been documented that when young children are ready to learn how to read, the learning of sign language can strengthen and increase oral language and literacy skills. It was observed that hearing children of deaf parents were often reading before they began school because their parents had fingerspelled with them. The researchers concluded that these children were able to make the connection between the manual letters of fingerspelling and the printed letters on a page. We have also learned a great deal about multiple intelligences from Howard Gardner—and the importance of understanding and identifying the wide variety of individual learning styles as well as the importance of multisensory teaching. Sign language involves seeing, hearing, and movement. This is the perfect combination of the ways young children learn best. Using the multisensory approaches of sign language, children are able to use both sides of the brain, thus creating multiple pathways which can strengthen memory and build connections for further learning.

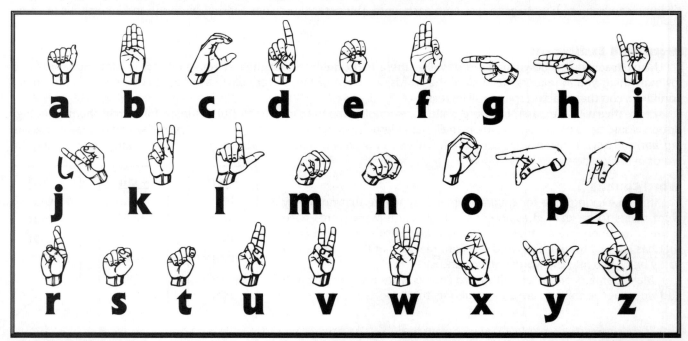

Spelling Strategies and Suggestions

Although spelling is often taught separately from the reading or phonics program, it is included here for these reasons. First, children with dyslexia struggle with spelling and probably will continue to experience spelling difficulties throughout their lifetimes. As part of their schooling, they will be expected to participate in classroom spelling instruction and take spelling tests. Next, spelling reinforces reading instruction and can help teach phonics skills—we spell by identifying sounds and writing those sounds as letters to make words. When reading, we look at words and letters and convert them into sounds. Ideally, spelling instruction should be connected to the reading program by creating spelling words from the current reading vocabulary.

The following are a variety of strategies, suggestions, and helpful hints that can make learning to spell more fun and more effective for your students with dyslexia.

Obvious and Often Necessary—Short Lists of Words

Reduce the number of words that a child is expected to learn how to spell. A short list of words based on current reading vocabulary or structure-based words will allow the student to be more successful. Two to four irregular words can also be included each week which can help improve writing skills.

Simultaneous Oral Spelling (SOS)

Simultaneous oral spelling is a multisensory technique that uses visual, auditory, and kinesthetic senses. This technique is used in the Orton-Gillingham methods to teach irregular sight words.

❑ **Auditory:** The teacher says the word and the child repeats it.

❑ **Visual and Auditory:** The child looks at the word, says it again, and then says each of the letters.

❑ **Visual, Auditory, and Kinesthetic:** The child looks at the word, says the word, says each of the letters, and then writes the word while saying each letter as it is written. Finally, the child says the whole word after it is written.

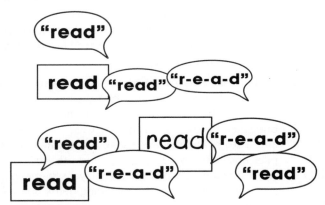

Spelling and Art

On the bottom of a sheet of paper, write a short phrase or sentence containing a spelling word. Then, have the child illustrate the phrase or sentence. The sillier the picture, the more memorable it will become. The picture will give the words meaning and relevant content. Ask the child to go back to the featured spelling word and say and spell it several times.

Large Print Spelling Cards

Use a computer to make spelling word flash cards—one word per card. Choose a plain font and a point size of 60, 72, or 90. Let children draw an illustration on the back of each word card. It may also help to highlight or use the computer to change the color of the letters or part of the word that is giving the child the most difficulty. For example in the word *could*, if the child has a difficult time remembering the *ou* in the middle of the word, then highlight the *ou* with a marker or make the *ou* a different color font on the flash card. Using both the illustration and the differing colors can help the child learn the word.

American Sign Language (ASL)

Finger spell featured spelling words using American Sign Language. This can be effective, and it is a lot of fun for the children. (See page 50 to read the research and as a reference for the ASL alphabet signs.)

Mnemonic Spelling

Mnemonic spelling is a memory technique that has been useful for many children with reading disabilities. It can be especially helpful for those children who have good auditory memories. Choose a difficult spelling word and come up with a silly phrase or rhyme. See the examples on the following page.:

Mnemonic spelling examples:

The—**T**en **h**ens **e**at!

Said—**S**he **a**lways **i**s **d**ancing.

Because—**B**ugs **e**at **c**arrots **a**nd **u**se **s**ilverware **e**asily.

What—**W**ild **h**orses **a**lways **t**rot.

Like—**L**ook **i**n **K**arl's **e**ngine.

Was—**W**ally **a**te **s**paghetti.

Here—**H**arry's **e**agle **r**arely **e**ats.

There—**T**he **h**uge **e**lephant **r**an **e**verywhere.

What—**W**ho **h**as **a** **t**reat?

Spelling Word Games

Spelling word games are both fun and effective for practicing and learning spelling words. You can easily create the following two games:

❏ **Concentration:** Make two flash cards for each spelling word. Place the cards in rows facedown on a table. Students take turns picking up two cards. Have the child read the words on the cards and spell each word. If they match, the child keeps the pair. If the cards do not match, they are replaced facedown on the table and play passes to the next player.

❏ **Lotto:** Make two game boards (see illustration) with one spelling word written in each game board square. Do not use all of the featured words on each board. Make two sets of game cards with one spelling word on each card. Give each player a game board and a set of cards. Players take turns drawing a card from their piles and reading and then spelling the word on the card. If the word matches a word on the player's game board, the player then puts that card on the matching game board square. The first player to fill up her game board is the winner.

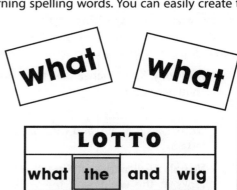

Word Families and Common Patterns

It is much easier to learn a new list of spelling words when the words on the list have something in common such as word families, prefixes and suffixes, or common medial sounds.

Teach Proofreading

Very often children with dyslexia do not seem to be able to notice and then correct their spelling errors. Teaching older children to proofread can be helpful. Encourage children to notice errors that they routinely make. By becoming aware of those errors, they are more likely to try to catch their own mistakes.

Improving Oral Reading and Fluency Skills

Children with dyslexia will have a much easier time learning how to read and build fluency when their reading experiences are positive. Remember, reading should be fun! Unfortunately, oral reading can be a painful experience for a child with dyslexia. These children should never be forced to read aloud in class. Being made to read aloud is probably the quickest way to discourage dyslexic children from ever wanting to work on their reading skills. Encourage reading aloud during quiet times with just you or the child's parent. It is often helpful to send home selected reading material so that children can practice oral reading with their parents.

Never ask children to read books that are beyond their ability levels. There is no enjoyment or any learning when children have to struggle with every word. Find books that are the appropriate reading level and have content that is extremely interesting to the child. The more interesting the content, the more the child will want to read it.

Also, learning to recognize high-frequency words and regular word patterns definitely increases fluency. Spend time helping the child learn the 100 most used words (see page 48). There are many other fun activities that can enrich a child's reading experience, build fluency, increase reading expression, and strengthen comprehension skills. Incorporate some of the following ideas into your lesson plans.

Choral Stories/Readers' Theatre

Choose a story that requires children to read a familiar part or where they can join together in saying a chorus, choral chant, or refrain in the appropriate places in the story. For example, while reading "The Three Pigs," the whole class could chorus, "Not by the hair on my chinny-chin-chin." After participating in the storytelling, the children will love to read the story on their own.

Overhead Reading

Have the whole class read a book together by using the overhead projector. The reading can be done aloud as a group, individually, or silently with the whole class enjoying the book at the same time. Circle the words that are new, or the words that children have difficulty decoding. Read and reread the story to increase fluency. When the children can read the text with ease, invite some children to act out the story while others read the pages aloud. In this way, the activity can become "story theatre."

Taped Reading

The use of books or selected texts recorded on tape can be extremely beneficial for the child with dyslexia. There are many ways to effectively use recorded text.

❑ **The teacher or parent can record a story or selected text with a tape recorder.** The child can first listen to the story or text and later can follow along, touching each word as it is read.

❑ **Purchase books with audio tapes to motivate students.** Children can listen to stories that are written above their current reading levels, and they will definitely benefit from hearing stories that are appropriate to their interest levels. For example, the Harry Potter series of books are enormously popular with children but are difficult books to read. Children with dyslexia will love these stories and they will increase their vocabulary and language skills. In addition, they will be able to discuss something popular with their peers.

❑ **Have the child record a story on the tape recorder.** First, have the child practice the text and then make the recording. Play back the recording so that the child can check his oral reading as he rereads the story silently. Listening to themselves read is an effective way to motivate children to practice their reading skills.

Watch the Reader

Have children in a reading group listen to you read. Ask them to follow along silently and catch any mistakes. Read slowly. Keep the children engaged by asking their help with words or by misreading every fifth word. Children will giggle over catching their teacher making a mistake, and at the same time, they will become more aware of accurate reading.

Unison Reading

Select a favorite story. Have one of the children who is a good reader read the story to the rest of the class, or have two children stand in front of the class and take turns reading while the other students follow along. It is also fun for the whole class to read in unison. This is a safe way for the child with dyslexia to practice oral reading without being fearful that mistakes will be heard. The children will have the thrill of performing and at the same time will receive practice in reading.

Paired Reading Tips

Children love being read to and taking turns reading. Encourage parents to sit with their children and read with them. Tell parents not to let their children stumble or spend too much time struggling to sound out a word—simply tell the child the missed word. In doing this, children will enjoy the story, better understand the content of the story, not become frustrated when they do not know a word, and will be able to practice their reading skills in a safe and motivational environment.

Look for Specific Words

While reading with a child, tell them that you will do most of the reading, but the child is to follow along and look for a specific word. For example, if you were reading the story "The Three Bears," stop each time you come to the word *bear*. It is the child's job to read the word *bear*. This helps the child focus and pay attention to all of the words that are being read.

Video and Books

It is wonderful for children of all ages, but especially for late elementary and middle school children, to watch a movie about a classic story before attempting to read it. Students will enjoy watching film adaptations of books like Anna Sewell's *Black Beauty*; Hans Christian Andersen's *The Snow Queen, The Little Mermaid, The Emperor's New Clothes*, and *The Princess and the Pea;* Louisa May Alcott's *Little Women;* Carlo Collodi's *The Adventures of Pinocchio;* Roald Dahl's *Charlie and the Chocolate Factory*; Esther Forbes's *Johnny Tremain;* Fred Gipson's *Old Yeller;* Kenneth Grahame's *The Wind in the Willows*; Grimms' Fairy Tales; E. B. White's *Stuart Little* and *Charlotte's Web*; C. S. Lewis' The Chronicles of Narnia series; Astrid Lingren's *Pippi Longstocking*; L. M. Montgomery's Anne of Green Gables series; Mary Norton's *Bed-Knob and Broomstick*; and many more.

Poetry Day

Set aside a day to enjoy poetry. Recommend books of poetry for children to read. Invite children to read aloud a favorite poem. After sharing their favorite poems, have children write their own couplets about a person, event, holiday, or object. Alternatively, give children the first line of a verse and ask them to make a rhyme for the second line. Duplicate their writings and give each child a copy. A better appreciation for poetry will be the result.

I like you!	You are my best friend,

And you like me, too!	For always, the end!

Children's Read Aloud and Poetry Book List

- ❏ *Abuela*. Arthur Dorros. (Dutton, 1991)
- ❏ *The Adventures of Taxi Dog*. Debra Barracca. (Dial, 1990)
- ❏ *Alison's Zinnia*. Anita Lobel. (Greenwillow, 1990)
- ❏ *Amelia's Road*. Linda Jacobs. (Altman, Lee & Low Books, 1995)
- ❏ *Animals Should Definitely Not Wear Clothing*. Judi Barrett. (Atheneum, 1970)
- ❏ *Anno's Counting House*. Mitsumasa Anno. (Philomel Books, 1982)
- ❏ *Araminta's Paint Box*. Karen Ackerman. (Atheneum, 1990)
- ❏ *Bearsie Bear and the Surprise Sleepover Party*. Bernard Waber. (Houghton Mifflin, 1997)
- ❏ *Blueberries for Sal*. Robert McCloskey. (Viking Books, 1976)
- ❏ *Brown Bear, Brown Bear, What Do You See?* Bill Martin Jr. (Henry Holt and Co., 1996)
- ❏ *Bunny Cakes*. Rosemary Wells. (Puffin Books, 2000)
- ❏ *Bunny Money*. Rosemary Wells. (Puffin Books, 2000)
- ❏ *Buz*. Richard Egielski. (HarperCollins Children's Books, 1995)
- ❏ *Cloudy with a Chance of Rain*. Judi Barret. (Aladdin, 1982)
- ❏ *The Chanukkah Guest*. Eric A. Kimmel. (Holiday House, 1990)
- ❏ *Charlotte's Web*. E. B. White. (HarperTrophy, 1974)
- ❏ *Chicka Chicka Boom Boom*. Bill Martin Jr. (Simon & Schuster, 1989)
- ❏ *Chicken Sunday*. Patricia Polacco. (Philomel Books, 1992)
- ❏ *Dinorella: A Prehistoric Fairy Tale*. Pamela Duncan Edwards. (Hyperion, 1997)
- ❏ *Elizabeth and Larry*. Marilyn Sadler. (Simon & Schuster, 1990)
- ❏ *Elmer*. David McKee. (HarperCollins, 1989)
- ❏ *Emily and the Enchanted Frog*. Helen V. Griffith. (Greenwillow, 1989)
- ❏ *Eppie M. Says*. Olivier Dunrea. (Simon & Schuster, 1990)
- ❏ *The Enormous Crocodile*. Roald Dahl. (Knopf Books, 2000)
- ❏ *Everybody Needs a Rock*. Byrd Baylor. (Atheneum, 1974)
- ❏ *Feathers for Lunch*. Lois Ehlert. (Harcourt, 1990)
- ❏ *First Day Jitters*. Julie Danneberg. (Charlesbridge Publishing, 2000)
- ❏ *Flossie and the Fox*. Patricia McKissack. (Dutton Books, 1986)
- ❏ *The Foot Book*. Dr. Seuss. (Random House, 1968)
- ❏ *Gathering the Sun: An Alphabet in Spanish and English*. Alma Flor Ada. (Rayo, 1997)
- ❏ *Give Me a Sign! What Pictograms Tell Us Without Words*. Tiphaine Samoyault. (Viking Books, 1997)
- ❏ *Good Driving, Amelia Bedelia*. Peggy Parish. (HarperTrophy, 1996)
- ❏ *Goodnight Moon*. Margaret Wise Brown. (HarperCollins, 1976)
- ❏ *The Great Kapok Tree*. Lynne Cherry. (Gulliver Green, 1990)
- ❏ *Green Eggs and Ham*. Dr. Seuss. (Random House, 1968)
- ❏ *The Grey Lady and the Strawberry Snatcher*. Molly Bang. (Simon & Schuster, 1984)
- ❏ *Growing Vegetable Soup*. Lois Ehlert. (Harcourt, 1987)
- ❏ *The Handmade Alphabet*. Laura Rankin. (Dial, 1991)
- ❏ *Hattie and the Fox*. Mem Fox. (Simon & Schuster, 1987)
- ❏ *Hello, Mrs. Piggle-Wiggle*. Betty MacDonald. (HarperCollins, 1957)
- ❏ *Hop on Pop*. Dr. Seuss. (Random House, 1976)
- ❏ *Horace*. Holly Keller. (Greenwillow, 1991)
- ❏ *I Do Not Want to Get Up Today*. Dorothy Cantor. (Little Brown and Company, 2001)
- ❏ *I Know an Old Lady Who Swallowed a Fly*. Simms Taback. (Viking, 1997)
- ❏ *If You Give a Moose a Muffin*. Laura Numeroff. (Laura Geringer, 1991)
- ❏ *The Important Book*. Margaret Wise Brown. (HarperTrophy, 1990)
- ❏ *In a Cabin in a Wood*. Darcie McNally. (Cobblehill, 1991)
- ❏ *In the Tall, Tall Grass*. Denise Fleming. (Henry Holt & Co., 1995)

- *James and the Giant Peach.* Roald Dahl. (Puffin, 2000)
- *Julius, the Baby of the World.* Kevin Henkes. (Greenwillow, 1990)
- *Knuffle Bunny: A Cautionary Tale.* Mo Willems. (Hyperion, 2004)
- *The Last Tales of Uncle Remus.* Julius Lester. (Dial Books, 1994)
- *Lester's Dog.* Karen Hesse. (Knopf Books, 1993)
- *The Little Engine That Could.* Watty Piper. (Grosset & Dunlap, 1978)
- *Little Pea.* Amy Krouse Rosenthal. (Chronicle Books, 2005)
- *Little Red Riding Hood: A Newfangled Prairie Tale.* Lisa Campbell Ernst. (Simon & Schuster, 1995)
- *Lon Po Po.* Ed Young. (Philomel Books, 1989)
- *Ma Dear's Aprons.* Patricia C. McKissack. (Atheneum, 1997)
- *Madeline.* Ludwig Bemelmans. (Viking, 1958)
- *Make Way for Ducklings.* Robert McCloskey. (Viking, 1941)
- *Millions of Cats.* Wanda Gág. (Rebound by Sagebrush, 1999)
- *Miss Rumphius.* Barbara Cooney. (Viking, 1982)
- *The Mitten.* Jan Brett. (Putnam Juvenile, 1989)
- *The Mixed-Up Chameleon.* Eric Carle. (HarperTrophy, 1988)
- *Mr. Popper's Penguins.* Richard Atwater. (Little Brown, 1988)
- *The Mud Flat Olympics.* James Stevenson. (Greenwillow Books, 1994)
- *My Memory String.* Eve Bunting. (Clarion Books, 2000)
- *My Painted House, My Friendly Chicken, and Me.* Maya Angelou. (Crown Books, 2003)
- *My Very First Mother Goose.* Iona Opie. (Candlewick, 1999)
- *Nana Upstairs, Nana Downstairs.* Tomie De Paola. (Putnam, 1975)
- *The Napping House.* Audrey and Don Wood. (Harcourt, 1984)
- *The New Adventures of Mother Goose.* Bruce Lansky. (Meadowbrook, 1993)
- *No, David!* David Shannon. (Scholastic, 1998)
- *Olivia.* Ian Falconer. (Atheneum, 2000)
- *Once Upon a Springtime.* Jean Marzollo. (Econo-Clad Books, 1999)
- *One Fish, Two Fish, Red Fish, Blue Fish.* Dr. Seuss. (Random House, 1976)
- *The Polar Express.* Chris Van Allsburg. (Houghton Mifflin, 1985)
- *The Red Balloon.* Albert Lamorisse. (Doubleday, 1967)
- *The Relatives Came.* Cynthia Rylant. (Aladdin, 1993)
- *The Snowy Day.* Ezra Jack Keats. (Viking, 1962)
- *Squirrels.* Brian Wildsmith. (Oxford University Press, 1992)
- *Stellaluna.* Janell Cannon. (Harcourt, 1993)
- *The Story of Babar.* Jean de Brunhof. (Random House, 1937)
- *The Story of Ferdinand.* Munro Leaf. (Viking, 1936)
- *Swimmy.* Leo Lionni. (Knopf Books, 1992)
- *The Three Little Pigs.* James Marshall. (Puffin Books, 1996)
- *This Is the House That Jack Built.* Pam Adams. (Child's Play-International, 1990)
- *Town Mouse, Country Mouse.* Jan Brett. (Putnam, 1994)
- *The 20th Century Children's Book Treasury: Picture Books and Stories to Read Aloud.* Janet Schulman. (Knopf, 1998)
- *26 Letters and 99 Cents.* Tana Hoban. (Greenwillow, 1987)
- *Two of Everything.* Lily Toy Hong. (Albert Whitman & Company, 1992)
- *What Do You Do with a Tail Like This?* Melinda Long. (Harcourt, 2003)
- *Why Mosquitoes Buzz in People's Ears.* Verna Aardema. (Dial, 1975)
- *The World That Jack Built.* Ruth Brown. (Dutton Books, 1991)

Increasing Comprehension

Grab Bag

Decorate a paper bag. Fill the bag with cards that represent four or five different events in a story the children have just finished reading. The cards can either be written sentences that describe the event or illustrated pictures of the events.

Have children take turns drawing a card out of the bag. Using a pocket chart or the ledge of the blackboard, the children should decide as a group how to properly sequence and arrange the cards to retell the story's events. When the small group of children have finished sequencing their cards, the rest the class may then decide whether the cards are in the correct order. Finally, have the small group of children retell the story using the sentence or picture cards as their guide.

Story Comics

After reading a story, have children make a four-panel comic strip that retells the important events in the story. Show the action of the characters and use balloons over their heads to indicate their speech. These comic strips can be duplicated and distributed to the class for fun reading.

Get a Glimpse of a Good Book

Ask children to each bring a shoe box to school. Trim drawing paper to fit inside one end of each box. Have children illustrate an interesting scene from the book they have just read and glue the drawings in place inside their boxes. Actual objects and cutouts can be added to the scenes to give them a 3-D effect. Have an adult cut a small hole approximately 1" (25 mm) in diameter in the end of the box opposite the drawing. Underneath the hole have the child print the book title and author's name. Then, cut a 1.5" (3.8 cm) wide slot across one end of the shoe box lid. Place the cover back on the box, making sure the slot is above the scene to allow in some light.

Children will enjoy peeking through the hole to view the scene at the back of each box. Display all of the "peek boxes" on a counter with the caption "Get a glimpse of a good book to read."

Room Reader

Choose a memorable character from a recent story and have the class make up new adventures for that character. Write down the children's ideas and then make copies of the new version for the class. This experience gives children an opportunity to reread the story they have written and helps them to gain a better understanding of the story and the story's vocabulary.

Big Book

Make an oversized book of a favorite story. Use heavy cardboard for the cover and inside pages. Choose a story that can be retold in about eight scenes and write on each page the story segment to be illustrated. Divide the class into eight groups—each group will create a page for the book. When finished, let the children decide how the pages should be sequenced before binding them together.

Rewrite the Ending

This activity can be completed in two different ways. First, have children fold an 8.5" x 11" (22 cm x 28 cm) paper in half. On the top half of the paper, have children illustrate the story's original ending. Then, on the bottom half of the page, have them complete one of two illustration ideas. Children can either write and illustrate a new ending from a certain point in the story, or they can start at the author's original ending, extend the story beyond the author's ending, and then illustrate the new ending.

Arranging Cards

After reading a favorite book to the class, ask children the question, "What is one thing that you remember from the story?" Accept all answers. Write the responses of 10 to 12 children on large index cards or sentence strips and then give the cards to those students.

Have the students bring their response cards to the front of the classroom. The children remaining in their seats must decide as a group how to arrange the answers in a meaningful way. There must be a consensus among the seated children. Any arrangement that makes sense, and that the group can defend, is acceptable.

"Map-It-Out"

Have the children draw a map of the setting for the story or of the main character's neighborhood, city, or room. For example, children might draw a map of the "100 Acre Wood" from A. A. Milne's *Winnie-the-Pooh*.

Take a Picture

Read a story to the children and then invite them to pretend that they are photographers. Explain that they will "take a picture" of the most important part of the story by drawing it. The children can add captions to explain what is happening in their "photographs."

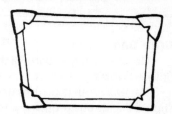

True or False?

Write statements—both true and false—about a selection the children have read. Prepare cards with the word *true* written on one side and the word *false* written on the other side. The cards may be laminated for durability. Give each child a card; children will respond to each statement you read by holding up their cards to vote whether they believe each statement is true or false.

TV Show

Announce to the children that they are going to create a television show from one of their reading selections. To begin, gather statements (one statement per child) that advance the plot of the story. Include the title page. Then, work together to organize the statements in proper sequence. Number the statements sequentially and hand back each child's statement for the child to illustrate.

Put all of the illustrations in order and tape them together to make one long strip. Tape the ends of the strip to cardboard tubes as shown in the illustration below. Have two children turn the tubes in unison so that the other children can watch their "TV show." You may choose a narrator to tell the story. To extend the activity, children may enjoy making a television from a cardboard box to "frame" the scrolling story illustrations.

Picture Book Murals

Divide the class into three or more groups. In their groups, encourage the children to write down 5 to 10 statements on sentence strips that tell the story of the chosen reading selection. Then, have them sequence the events and glue them in order onto a large piece of butcher paper. When the children have finished this, they may draw illustrations above the statements.

Alternatively, you may wish to complete the activity by helping children to generate the story statements. Then, each group will sequence and illustrate the same statements. As another option, younger children can illustrate and then verbally describe to you what is happening in their pictures.

Casting Director

After children have read the story, ask them to list all of the characters and discuss the characters' attributes and personalities. This can be done individually or as a class activity.

Choose several students to serve as casting directors. The directors will cast the members of their class into the roles of the characters from the story. If appropriate, the casting directors could try to cast children according to similarities they may share with the story's characters.

Those children cast as characters might then enjoy trying to dramatize a scene or event from the story.

Postreading Strategies—Page 62

After reading a story, complete several of the strategies below to help students recall, understand, and analyze what they read.

❑ Make a vocabulary list of the new words from the story.

❑ Discuss: Was the story easy to read? Was it difficult to understand, or was it just right?

❑ Complete the first two columns of the KWL chart (as shown) before reading the story. Then, fill in the column "L—What I Learned" after reading the story.

❑ Direct children to go back and reread the sections that they may have had difficulty with while reading the first time.

❑ Discuss: Did the children like story? Did they find it interesting? What might they want to change in the story?

KWL Chart

What I **K**now	**W**What I ant to know.	What I **L**earned.

Postcard

Copy the postcard pattern (below) onto card stock, one per child. Have each child write a short note on the postcard: to a friend to persuade the friend to read the story; to a movie producer to convince him to make a movie of the story; or to the author to share what the student liked about the story. Invite children to draw appropriate illustrations on the front of their postcards.

Developing Writing Skills
and Motivating Children to Write

Children with dyslexia often have wonderful imaginations, which are an asset for helping children to become interested in writing. Because most of these children will struggle with spelling, punctuation, handwriting, and the ability to sequence their ideas, it is important to teach them that writing is a two-part process. The first part is coming up with "writing ideas" and getting those ideas down on paper. The second part is when the writer goes back to edit and correct what he has written.

The Very Beginning—A Picture Is Worth a Thousand Words

Books that have no words, just beautiful illustrations, can provide wonderful early writing and visual learning experiences. Sit with the children, page through a wordless book, and let them put their own words to the story. Creating their own stories stimulates imagination and increases language skills.

As children progress and begin to actually write some words, let them create their own books. Cut out pictures from magazines and coloring books, glue the pictures to blank pages, and invite children to write sentences to go with the pictures. Children can also have great fun cutting words out of newspapers and magazines and arranging them into short sentences to go with the illustrations. Have them glue the words in proper sequence under each picture.

Journal and Writing Prompts

Let children decorate journals or storybooks or have them make their own. For each of the children's journals or books, choose writing paper with the appropriate line width (kindergarten or primary widths), number of lines per page, size of illustration boxes, and number of pages. Struggling writers may only want a few pages with two writing lines, whereas older students, or children with progressing skills, may want journals filled with many pages.

Provide children with various journal prompts to help them get started writing. Add praise and positive comments to what the children have written. Remember, the purpose of journal writing is to provide meaningful writing practice about topics that interest and motivate young writers.

Ideas for Journal Prompts

- The happiest time of my life . . .
- One question I would like to ask . . .
- If I could live anywhere, it would be . . .
- The scariest dream I ever had . . .
- If I had a million dollars, I would . . .
- I think this rule is unfair because . . .
- My greatest adventure ever was . . .
- I knew the seed was magic when . . .
- My favorite sandwich is . . .
- I am the happiest when . . .
- Look what lives in outer space . . .
- I want to tell you about my friend . . .
- The biggest mess I ever made . . .
- I like being a boy/girl because . . .

- I wish that I could . . .
- When I turn 16 years old . . .
- I very much dislike . . .
- My hero is . . .
- The worst thing ever . . .
- When I grow up . . .
- I see bugs everywhere . . .
- I would like to make . . .
- I saw a dinosaur in my . . .
- I get upset when . . .
- My favorite memory is . . .
- I do not like to . . .
- I held the magic wand and . . .
- It really scares me when . . .

- My future wife/husband . . .
- My favorite story is . . .
- I am really bothered by . . .
- My heart beats faster when . . .
- If I could fly, I would travel to . . .
- My toys can talk . . .
- The biggest thing I ever saw . . .
- This summer I want to . . .
- If I had a superhero power . . .
- I saw a very strange . . .
- I really don't like this food . . .
- I would pack in my suitcase . . .
- This weekend I am going to . . .
- If I had a camera, I would . . .

Make Writing Reference Materials—*My Own Spelling Book*

My Own Spelling Book is meant to be used as a dictionary. Staple together 26 pages to form a booklet—one page for each letter of the alphabet. Have the children write down words that they use frequently and words that are of interest to them. This book will serve as a growing reference tool to help children with their writing activities. Some students may need to draw pictures next to new words to help them remember the words' meanings.

It may be helpful to preprint the 26 letter pages and include sight words and other words that students will need to know and use in their writing throughout the year. Use the sight words listed on page 48 as a reference.

Find-the-Page Race Alphabetizing Game: Go though the pages of *My Own Spelling Book* with students. Talk about the fact that pages are organized alphabetically. Play a "find-the-page" race to help students become more familiar with alphabetizing. Say the name of a letter, such as *M*. The children then race as fast as they can to find the *M* page in their books. Children should raise their hands once they have found the requested page. The first child to find the page chooses a new letter for the class to find.

The Value of Graphic Organizers—Pages 62 through 67

A graphic organizer is a visual display that can help students with language processing deficits by visually presenting the most important information and eliminating the information that is less important. Students may also use graphic organizers to sequence their thoughts, which can stimulate their writing. See pages 62–67 for some reproducible graphic organizers that will help your students improve their writing skills.

Two full-color graphic organizer transparencies have been included in the back of this book: Spider Writing Web and Story Organizer.

The Writing Process Using a Story or Web Graphic Organizer

1. Prewriting
Have students write down their ideas using a story or web graphic organizer.

2. Drafting
Have students write first drafts using their graphic organizers as a guide.

3. Revising
When the first drafts are complete, have students look over their work and decide where revisions should be made. Ask each student if all of the sentences relate to the topic. Also, ask if he thinks that anyone reading the work would understand it.

4. Editing
Have students write final drafts, making sure that each sentence begins with a capital letter and that the ending punctuation is correct.

5. Sharing
The students' work is "published" and shared with others (friends, classmates, parents, another teacher, etc.). A published work can include a book, a paper, a paper with an accompanying art project, or an electronic file.

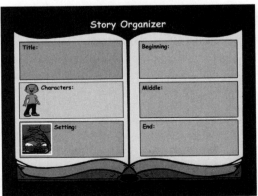

What I **K**now	**W**hat I ant to know.	What I **L**earned.

Directions: Draw pictures or write words to help remember sequential events in the story.

STORYBOARD

1.	2.	3.
4.	5.	6.

Name

The Who, What, When, Where, and Why Reporter

○ Who was in the story?

What happened?

○ When did it happen?

Where did it happen?

○ Why did it happen?

Teaching Tips for Kids with Dyslexia

Name

Main Idea
Ice Cream Cone

Directions: Write the title and main idea on the cone. Write a supporting detail in each scoop of ice cream.

KE-804059 © Key Education

Name

Star Maps

Directions: This is one of the most versatile organizers.

1. Story Character. Write the character's name in the center of the star and then write descriptive words about the character in the star's points.

2. Main Idea. Write the main idea in the center of the star and the supporting details in the star's points.

Name

Detailed Character Map

Directions: Have each child list three of the character's personality traits in the rectangular boxes. Then have them justify their choices by identifying the character's actions, ideas, words, and feelings that support those chosen traits. The children can record that specific information in the oval shapes.

☐ Write the name of the character.

▭ Write words that describe the character.

⬭ How did the character show those qualities?

Teaching Tips for Kids with Dyslexia

KE-804059 © Key Education

Cute Kid
Character Map

Directions: Direct the children to write the name of the character on the baseball cap and then fill in each body section with a few short words or phrases that describe the character's personality.

Comic Talk!

Directions: Draw two characters and write a short conversation, joke, or riddle.

Teaching Tips for Kids with Dyslexia

KE-804059 © Key Education

The Story Racetrack

Write about what happened in the beginning, the middle, and the end of the story.

Name: _____

Title of story _____

This is the beginning.

This is the middle.

This is the end.

The Comparing and Contrasting Ladybug

Directions: Use to help the children identify similarities and differences in fictional characters, cultures, science topics, and so on. On the ladybug's wings the children can write the name of the topic or character and explain how each subject differs. In the section at the ladybug's bottom, each child can list words that tell how the subjects are similar.

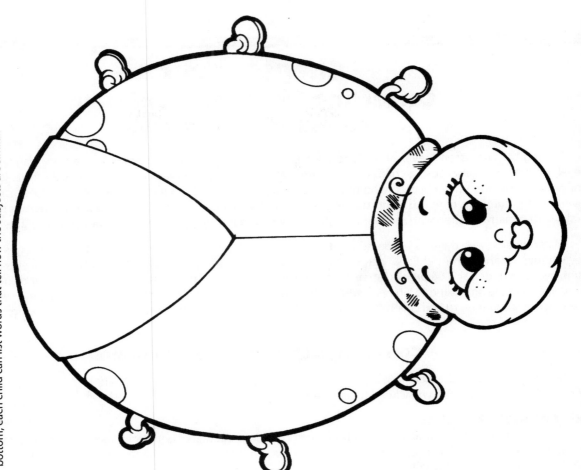

Teaching Tips for Kids with Dyslexia

Story Pyramid

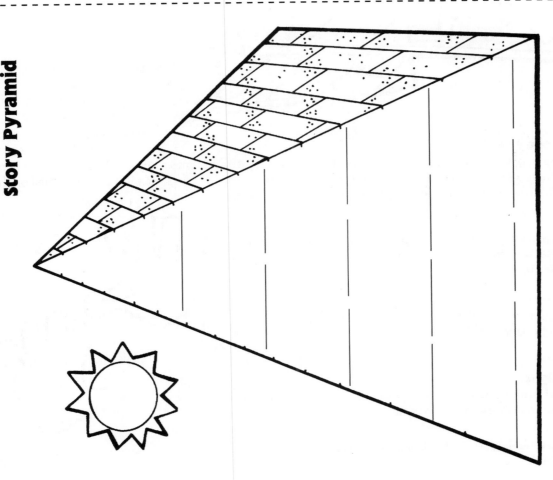

Line 1: Write the name of a character.

Line 2: Write 2 words that tell about the setting.

Line 3: Write 3 words that tell about the character.

Line 4: Write 4 words that tell about one event in the story.

Line 5: Write 5 words in a sentence that tells about the ending of the story.

KE-804059 © Key Education

Chapter Four
Correcting Left/Right Confusion and Handwriting Tips

Writing backwards, and reversals of letters and small words, are actually common in the early stages of handwriting development. Simply because a child reverses some letters does not mean that the child has dyslexia. It is also equally important to mention that children who have dyslexia, or other related reading disabilities, do not necessarily reverse or invert letters, numbers, or words. Unfortunately, so many people have believed that reversals are part of the problems of dyslexia that many children with reading disabilities have not been diagnosed because they print accurately.

Many children with dyslexia will demonstrate some of the following problems that can create challenges with fine motor development. Many of these children demonstrate confusion with directional words and positional concepts such as left and right, over and under, and before and after. Many of these children are late to establish a dominant hand and may continue switching from the right hand to left hand while coloring, writing, or doing any other motor task until they are 7 or 8 years old. Even then, it is common to find children who may use one hand for writing and the other hand for throwing.

Correcting Left from Right Confusion

Many children with dyslexia have a difficult time understanding the concepts of "left" and "right." The following ideas will provide the help children may need to learn left from right.

Left and Right Bracelets
Let each of the children make construction paper bracelets, decorated with letter reminders of "L" on the left-handed bracelet and reminders of "R" on the right-handed bracelet. Another idea is for children to wear a bracelet only on the hand that they automatically write with.

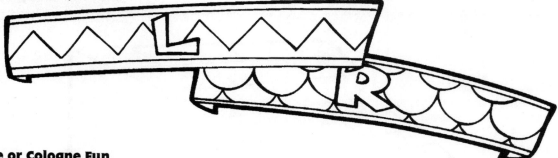

Perfume or Cologne Fun
After children are beginning to understand the concepts of left and right, sometimes a tiny bit of perfume or cologne on only one wrist can be a helpful reminder. You can put a LOVELY smell on the LEFT wrist or a REALLY NICE smell on the RIGHT wrist. Note: Check for allergies before using fragrances in the classroom.

Trace Hands
Trace the child's hand on card stock and label each hand with an "L" and an "R." Show the child that the pointer finger and the thumb on the left hand form the letter "L" when held up.

Play Simon Says
Play Simon Says and have the children "touch their right feet; raise their left hands; shake their right hands; shake their left hands, etc. Lots of fun practice can be helpful.

Tracing Left to Right
Tracing lines and connecting dots from left to right is good practice for learning that we read and write from left to right .

Teaching Cursive Writing is Often Recommended

There are many reasons why children with dyslexia often have difficulty with handwriting. Fortunately, there are some effective solutions to help these students conquer handwriting problems. First, let's look at why handwriting can be challenging.

Dysgraphia

Not all children with dyslexia, but some, will have additional learning challenges, such as dysgraphia—which literally means "difficulty with writing." Some experts believe that dysgraphia involves a dysfunction in the interaction between the two main brain systems that allow a person to translate mental into written language (sound to symbol, as well as mental word to written word). Other studies have shown that split attention, memory load, and familiarity of graphic material affect writing ability. Children who have dysgraphia may complain of cramped fingers while writing, erase excessively, write words backwards, experience trouble in sequencing the letters in words, have inconsistent letter formation, use a mixture of uppercase and lowercase letters, and their handwriting may be totally illegible. If you suspect dysgraphia, a more comprehensive multisensory therapy plan will be needed, and more than likely the child will eventually need to use a computer and word processing program when working on writing skills.

Multisensory Handwriting Practice

Often children with illegible handwriting have a combination of problems such as the inability to revisualize letters, and the inability to remember the motor patterns of letter forms. Fine and large motor activities can be extremely beneficial when practicing handwriting. Here are some easy-to-implement suggestions:

- ❏ Use a fingertip and practice on sandpaper.
- ❏ Fill a cookie sheet with sand or rice and then practice printing letters and words.
- ❏ Using a straight arm and pointed finger, pretend to write letters in the air (often called "sky-writing").
- ❏ Practice handwriting on a chalkboard using a paintbrush and water.
- ❏ Fingerpaint letters and words. Add glitter or salt to the paint to add an additional texture.
- ❏ Add various scents, such as mint or lemon extract, to fingerpaint to add the sense of smell.
- ❏ Print letters and words on paper plates using edible substances, such as yogurt, peanut butter, and pudding.

Decoding Difficulties Interfere with the Automatic Flow of Writing

When children learn how to read, they first have to be able to connect letters to sounds and then understand that letters represent the sounds in written language. When it comes to writing, children must be able to recreate words back onto paper. For children with dyslexia, decoding and making these connections is difficult, which can interfere with the automatic flow of writing.

Continuous Cursive is Often Recommended

In kindergarten, young children are typically taught how to "print." Then, when they reach the end of second grade, or in the beginning of third grade, children are taught cursive writing. Learning how to print and then having to switch to cursive handwriting creates another level of difficulty that can cause confusion. Being taught one method of handwriting is often better for children with dyslexia. Continuous cursive handwriting is often recommend as the preferred handwriting system for children with dyslexia. This is when every letter in a word is joined together and formed in one continuous movement without taking the pencil off the paper.

Continuous cursive can be helpful because:

- ❏ The continuous movement of cursive writing can decrease sequencing difficulties .
- ❏ By using continuous movement, a child can develop a "physical memory" of the word.
- ❏ Children are less likely to reverse letters which are typically difficult, such as "b and d" or "p and q," because of using continuous movement.
- ❏ There is a clearer distinction between uppercase and lowercase letters.
- ❏ The continuous flow of writing can eventually improve speed and spelling.

Handwriting Tips for Right-Handed Children

❑ **Maintain Good Posture.** Feet should be on the floor and the desk surface should be at a height for the arm and elbow to rest comfortably. Ankles, hips, and knees should all be at 90 degree angles. If the chair is too high, place a foot stool under the child's feet.

❑ **Slanted Surface.** Place a 4-inch three ring-binder on the desk in front of the child can sometimes be helpful. The spine of the binder should be facing the top of the desk. Rotate the binder to a 45 degree angle. Tape a piece of writing paper on the binder. Writing on this slanted surface is fun and can be extremely beneficial.

❑ **Align Paper.** Be sure that the paper is aligned parallel to the arm of the dominant hand and is at a 45 degree angle. The left hand should be used to hold the paper stable.

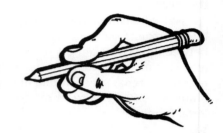

❑ **Proper Pencil Grasp.** The pencil should be held between the pads of the thumb and the index finger while resting on the middle finger. Another appropriate version of this grasp is for the pencil to be held between the pads of the thumb and the index and middle fingers while resting on the ring finger.

Extra Helpful Tips:

❑ **Pencil Grips.** Use pencil grips for children who have a difficult time remembering how to hold their pencil.

❑ **Short Pencils.** Break or sharpen pencils down to about a 2-inch length. This will encourage small hands to hold the pencil properly.

❑ **Chubby Writing Tools.** Use sidewalk chalk, chubby crayons, or a chubby pencil cut down to a short 2-inch length to help children gain more control.

Right-Handed Letter Formation Chart & Sequence of Letter Introduction

Little Letters—Swing Up and Down

							Little Letters (with a tail)

i   t   u   w   r   s   p   j

Little Round Letters—Swing Up, Curve Over, and Down   Little Hill Letters—Swing Up, Over, and Down

Little Round Letters (with a tail)

c   o   a   d   g   q   n   m   v   x

Little Tall Letters— Swing Up and Back Around Letters

Little Hill Letters (with a tail)

y   z   e   l   h   b   k   f

Big Round Letters   Big Flagpole Letters

C   A   O   E   N   M   K   H

Big Letters with a Ball   Big Snake Letters

P   B   R   U   W   Y   V   X

Big Letters with a Hat   Big Curly Letters

T   F   Z   2   I   J   G   S   L   D

Handwriting Tips for Left-Handed Children

Left-handed people have many more challenges in learning how to write. First, the English language requires that we write from left to right—just like we read. This writing direction allows the right-handed writer to "pull" the pencil away from the body and moves fluently across the paper. The left-handed writer must "push" the pencil as the arm moves towards and across the body. Many left-handed people find themselves holding their pencils in a "hooked" position as they write. This "hooked" position generally occurs because what they are writing is hidden by their writing hand, and so that they do not smear their own writing. This handwriting style is not correct, can be physically uncomfortable, and can even lead to messy or even illegible handwriting. Left-handed children need to be carefully TAUGHT how to write (or retaught), taking into consideration the unique differences when writing with a left-hand. (See illustrations below.)

- ❏ **Maintain Good Posture.** (Same as on page 70.)
- ❏ **Proper Pencil Grasp.** The pencil should be held between the pads of the thumb and the index finger while resting on the middle finger—approximately 1" (2 cm) to 1.5" (3.8 cm) from the point of the pencil.
- ❏ **Align Paper.** The paper is slanted (about 20%) to the right —although this can vary depending on comfort.
- ❏ **Arm, Wrist, and Hand Position.** The wrist should be straight and below the writing line. The arm should be almost parallel with the paper.
- ❏ **Handwriting Slant.** The cursive letter slant usually taught is difficult for left-handed students. It is more natural and more comfortable for left-handed students to write letters using an upright slant or even slanting their letters slightly to the left (See Left-Handed Writing Chart below.).

Left-Handed Letter Formation Chart & Sequence of Letter Introduction

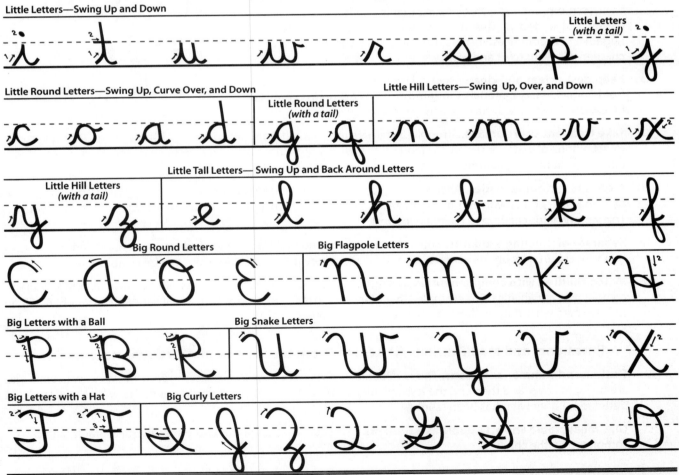

Chapter Five
Extra Tips for Helping Children with Dyslexia Become Successful Students

Classroom Accommodations and Material Modifications

Every classroom—in every state and province—has student populations of great diversity: diversity in learning styles, in academic abilities, in students' interest levels, and in students' home lives and cultural backgrounds. Every classroom will have children who need special attention and will benefit from teachers who take the time to make certain accommodations and modifications in the classroom.

Not all techniques and methods work with all children. Often it is a process of trial and error to discover what are the most successful techniques for individual students. The following classroom-tested suggestions have been found to be valuable for assisting teachers in managing a variety of special education needs and for helping young learners experience greater success in the regular education classroom.

Adjustments and Modifications for Schedules, Student Groups, Room Arrangement, and Classroom Work Space

- **Praise frequently.** All children are willing to work harder and will respond much better when they have consistent and honest praise and encouragement.

- **Stay close.** Early in the year, have these children sit closer to you for more positive feedback and to ensure that they have a clear understanding of assignments and expectations.

- **Provide quiet work areas.** Establish a quiet corner somewhere in the classroom, such as a study carrel, that is free from all distractions (visual and auditory). This space should never be associated with negative consequences. Instead, it should be a special place where children will want to sit and work.

- **Keep desks clear and clean.** Help children learn to keep their desks free of unnecessary materials. Cluttered desks create undue confusion for children who already have difficulty organizing materials.

- **Take frequent short breaks.** Struggling learners may benefit from taking frequent short breaks. A few seconds to get a drink of water or simply to stand up and walk around the room can be refreshing for children who find it difficult to sit for long periods of time.

- **Alternate various activities.** Alternate the types of activities and lessons presented in the classroom. For example, plan an activity that involves movement and active participation and then follow that lesson with a quiet activity. This variety helps children to maintain interest.

- **Separate distracting students.** Separate struggling students from other students who may be distracting to them. Sit children by others who can be helpful and where positive relationships can be established.

- **Match children with complementary strengths.** Pair children into "work teams" where partners bring different, complementary abilities. For example, an auditory learner could work with a visual learner. The children will be able to share what they are best at while helping each other.

Adjustments and Modifications for Lesson Presentation and Instructional Materials

- **Outline and summarize lessons.** This is valuable for the entire class. Begin a lesson with an overview of what you are going to cover and then end the lesson with a summary of what was accomplished. This will help all students better remember what has been taught.

- **Give measurable and attainable assignments.** Make sure that assignments are specific, measurable, and can be completed by the child.

❏ **Provide shorter assignments and work periods.** Shorter assignments and shorter work periods can give children a sense of completion and success. As children become more confident as learners, the length of both assignments and work periods can increase.

❏ **Reduce or eliminate spelling lists.** The best spelling lists are those that are sequential and based on reading lessons. Regular classroom lists are generally too long and may not relate directly to the child's reading instruction. Either eliminate the lists or use word lists that will be meaningful.

❏ **Provide the child with an enlarged photocopy of text.** Larger type is simply easier to read and looks less intimidating.

❏ **Copy chapters of textbooks and/or provide students with two copies of assignments.** Having copies allows the child the opportunity to underline, highlight, and make notes right on the assignment.

❏ **Cut or fold papers in half.** Students can easily be overwhelmed by assignments that appear to be long or overly crowded. Many children even appreciate receiving papers that are folded into fourths. It is rewarding for the student to feel as if she has completed something before moving onto the next task.

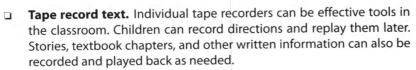

❏ **Use graph paper.** The use of graph paper works well for organizing mathematical problems and for writing out spelling words.

❏ **Don't force oral reading.** As mentioned earlier, children with dyslexia should never be forced to read aloud. If for some reason reading aloud is absolutely necessary, make sure that the child is told in advance and that he has been provided time to practice.

❏ **Provide as many visual, auditory, and tactile representations as possible.** Multisensory techniques will connect the brain's pathways and provide for more optimal learning experiences.

❏ **Improve organizational skills.** Encourage all students in your class to keep their work organized in folders.

❏ **Grading the child's work.** Nothing is more discouraging that getting back an assignment that is covered with red check marks! For a child who makes many mistakes, try circling in blue all of the words that are spelled correctly—emphasize what was done right. Note mistakes by discussing them with the child or by making a small dot by each error.

❏ **Computers and word processors.** Encourage children to become comfortable and proficient with using a word processor application. Children with handwriting difficulties, as well as visual learners, find word processors to be very effective teaching aids.

❏ **Tape record text.** Individual tape recorders can be effective tools in the classroom. Children can record directions and replay them later. Stories, textbook chapters, and other written information can also be recorded and played back as needed.

❏ **Let children take turns drilling each other.** This creates a nice social interaction and allows the auditory learner to speak and hear the information.

❏ **Have students make their own recordings.** Students can record their own information into a tape recorder. This provides children with important information that can be played again, and it gives them the opportunity to hear themselves speak the information, which helps children to internalize what they are learning.

❏ **Print flash cards in bright colors.** These are fun and can make the work more interesting.

❏ **Provide visual clues.** Use visual clues for all directions and information. Make frequent use of the chalkboard or wipe-off board.

❏ **Have students use self-stick adhesive notes.** These can be a valuable tool for visual learners. Encourage note taking and then have students stick the notes near the needed information. Self-stick notes also make great visual reminders of tasks that need to be completed, such as daily homework assignments.

Read pages 1–7
Math, page 24,
problems 1–10

❑ **Provide graphic organizers.** Graphic organizers can be useful for helping children organize and remember information. (See pages 61–67.)

❑ **Vary paper-and-pencil tasks.** Visual learners respond well to completing tasks that utilize a variety of art materials: crayons, cut-and-paste materials, magazine and newspaper collages, and colored pencils are just a few examples.

❑ **Provide alternatives to replace paper-and-pencil tasks.** The following are some alternative learning suggestions:

audio tapes	dramatizations	hands-on games	play dough	simulations
brainstorming	field trips	magnetic boards	poetry	tactile flash cards
bulletin boards	films	magnetic letters	posters	tape recorders
CD players	filmstrips	models	puppets	transparencies
chalkboards	flannel boards	oral presentations	read aloud books	videotapes
comic books	flip charts	overhead projectors	real objects	wipe-off boards
computers	glitter glue	peer tutors	role-playing	
displays	graphic organizers	photographs	sand trays	

Specific Adjustments and Modifications for Testing and Evaluations

❑ **Hold frequent conferences with children.** Let them know where they are succeeding and what areas still need work. Allow the child time to ask questions and talk about areas of frustration.

❑ **Underline the key direction words on tests.** Oftentimes, children do not complete their work correctly because they have misread or misunderstood the directions.

❑ **Do not time the tests.** Children work better without the pressure of being timed.

❑ **Allow these students to take tests in small sections over an extended period of time.** Children with dyslexia will need extra time for reading, rewriting, and proofreading their work.

❑ **Allow for flexible sitting.** Many children work better alone and without distractions.

❑ **Be aware of the difficulties of multiple-choice response testing.** Children with dyslexia often do poorly on multiple-choice response tests due to the large amount of reading required.

❑ **Allow oral examinations.** Children with dyslexia are often able to verbally demonstrate to the teacher all that they know about the subject matter.

❑ **Use alternative assessment methods.** Allow oral presentations, computer generated presentations, special projects, multimedia assignments, art projects, etc. Help children find alternative ways to present their knowledge through media and methods that will showcase their strengths.

Building Confidence and Motivation

It would be neglectful to fail to address the fact that many school-age children with dyslexia experience a lack of self-confidence. Children with dyslexia frequently believe that they are not as smart as their classmates, which creates a lack of confidence that can hinder learning. Children with dyslexia need to understand that they are as bright as their peers and very often have exceptional skills in other areas such as athletics, dramatics, art, or music. Here are some ideas to foster self-confidence in your students.

Compare and Contrast Weaknesses and Strengths

Together with the child, generate a list of his strengths and a list of weaknesses. The child will soon see that the list of strengths is far greater than the list of weaknesses. Send the list home to parents and ask them to add to the lists (especially to the list of their child's strengths.)

Give Nonacademic Classroom Awards

Children with dyslexia do not often receive school awards. Make sure that you give out awards for a variety of successes, such as having a clean desk, helping others, being a good friend, achieving in athletics, completing homework, etc. An award in one area can boost confidence in all school areas!

Give the Child Information about Dyslexia

The most important thing you can do is teach children that people with dyslexia are smart; they simply have a different learning style. Here are some literature resources to share with children:

- ❑ Betancourt, Jeanne. *My Name Is Brain Brian*. (Scholastic, 1996). This story about a 12-year-old boy's struggles with dyslexia is written with empathy and understanding.
- ❑ Robb, Diane Burton. *The Alphabet War: A Story about Dyslexia*. (Albert Whitman & Company, 2004). Adam used to love books, but when he enters school, his love of books becomes a daily battle. Finally diagnosed with dyslexia, Adam receives the help he needs and learns to how to read.
- ❑ Polacco, Patricia. *Thank You, Mr. Falker*. (Philomel Books, 2001). The author/illustrator shares her story about overcoming dyslexia and becoming a writer!

Homework Helpers

Children with dyslexia often arrive home at the end of the day and are not sure what their homework assignments are. This creates confusion for the child and is frustrating for parents. No one is quite sure of what the evening's homework entails. This generally happens because copying from the board is a difficult task for children with dyslexia. The following are some ideas that will make the process of completing homework easier for everyone.

At School Ideas for Teachers

- ❑ **Have a special space on the board for homework assignments.** Always write the homework assignments on the same place on the board and in large print. The child with dyslexia will know that he is copying the correct words.

- ❑ **Leave homework on the board all day.** Put the assignment on the board first thing in the morning and leave it up all day long. This ensures that the child has had enough time to copy down the assignment.

- ❑ **Use homework journals.** Every student should have a homework journal where assignments are written down. Before dismissal, quickly check everyone's journal to ensure that the assignments were copied correctly.

- ❑ **Strategically place the student's desk.** Be sure the dyslexic child's desk is close to the board so that the child can easily see it.

- ❑ **Provide homework handouts.** Homework handouts will benefit those students who are overly challenged by copying from the board.

- ❑ **Utilize the school's Web site.** If your school has a Web site where homework assignments can be posted daily, make sure that all students and their families are aware of this resource.

Homework Helpers for Parents

❏ **Use an assignment planner.** This simple system will help your child remember to bring assignments home. Include a reward system for using the assignment planner.

❏ **Call homework friends.** Have your child write down the names and phone numbers of a few reliable classmates. If the homework assignments are unclear, a friend can be called to clarify the night's assignments.

❏ **Establish a scheduled time for homework.** Determine a regular time when homework is to be done. Children will quickly get into the habit of doing homework on time.

❏ **Establish an organized place where homework can be completed.** Make sure this space is free of distractions—no TV, phone, or people coming and going.

❏ **Have readily available supplies.** Make sure that your child has everything that may be needed when it's time to begin homework: sharpened pencils, paper, crayons, ruler, and whatever special tools might be required for the assignments.

❏ **Get organized.** Teach your child to use an organizer. Develop a system for storing school papers and keeping them organized. Fewer materials will become misplaced or lost!

❏ **Have a snack.** Children who are hungry cannot concentrate as well. Make sure that your child has had a nutritious snack before beginning the homework.

❏ **Keep old quizzes and tests.** Old quizzes and tests can become valuable tools for your child when studying for a new test or for reviewing end-of-chapter material.

❏ **Be positive.** Completing homework can give children a sense of accomplishment and help them to feel successful. Establish a positive reward system.

❏ **Review the assignments with your child and help prioritize tasks.** Teach your child to review what has to be accomplished before beginning to do the homework. This helps children set priorities. It is often best for children to complete the work that is considered "hard" first. Save the "easy" homework for last.

❏ **Be available.** It is not your job to do your child's homework. However, you should be available to answer questions and provide guidance when needed.

❏ **Watch for failure or frustration.** Talk with your child's teacher immediately if you see that your child does not understand the assignments or is becoming frustrated or is not able to do the work without a large amount of assistance.

❏ **Check your child's assignments when finished.** This will allow you to see if your child is understanding the work that is being required. It will also make your child feel very proud when you look at the work and praise the accomplishments!

❏ **Keep in touch with your child's teacher.** Make sure there is regular communication between home and school.

❏ **Be aware of great trouble with reading.** If your child has a difficult time reading the material required, ask the teacher about recording the text on tape for your child to listen to at home. You can also read the material with your child to improve reading skills.

❏ **Homework should not go on all night.** If homework is taking too long, talk to the teacher. Hours and hours of homework is not beneficial for a young child!

Activities and Tips to Motivate Reading

Struggling readers need a stimulating environment and activities that are interesting, engaging, and designed to help the child experience success. This can be accomplished by first interrupting the cycle of failure, or with very young children by not letting the cycle ever begin. Break down the lessons into manageable segments; provide children with assignment choices; incorporate their personal interests into lessons; and focus on progress. These activities will show children that reading can be fun and that they can also be successful readers!

Book Clubs

Organize a classroom book club. Membership is open to the whole class. Select a President to call the roll and a Secretary to record the book read at each meeting. Decide on a book club name and make paper badges or hats with the club name on it that everyone can wear at the meetings. The members can vote on the book they want to read or have read to them. On the day of the meeting, the password to enter the club room may be the name of the book to be read that day. A discussion of the book and other related activities could follow. They could discuss illustrations, compare this book with others, suggest other books on the same subject, or pantomime the story. Clubs are simply excellent reading stimulators.

Reading Honor Roll Bulletin Board

Take a black and white close-up photograph of each child in the class. Place a caption on the bulletin board that says "We Are Honor Roll Readers." Every child's picture goes up on the bulletin board. The children will then get to earn stickers to be placed next to their photographs. To earn a sticker a child must keep a personal reading log. This reading log records the books that the **child has read at home** or **books that the parents have read to the child**. Set a goal that is appropriate for your class. Check reading logs weekly and then add the earned stickers to the bulletin board.

Balloon Burst

Obtain a large balloon for each reading group and enough small balloons so that each child in the room gets one. Duplicate a short list of books to be read by each of the reading groups. Prepare enough copies so that each child gets one. Roll the lists into small enough balls to insert into the large balloon. Inflate the balloon and suspend it from the ceiling where the reading groups meet. Repeat this step for each reading group.

When each group comes to the reading circle, a child is selected to stick a pin in the balloon. When it pops, each child in the reading group scrambles for a copy of the list. Make a chart of the book titles. Each time a child reads one of the listed books, they should receive a small balloon.

Story Time Serial

Take a long story or a book and read a part of it out loud each day. (See pages 45–46 for a list of Great Read-Aloud Books) Stop reading at a particularly exciting point in the story. Exclamations of disappointment will follow, but excitement will precede the next session. The whole idea is to leave the children wanting to hear more of the story. The children will hardly be able to wait for the book to be finished and placed on the library table for them to read.

To make this activity even more exciting, the teacher can add props as she reads the story. For example, if the story involves a princess, the teacher could wear a tiara. When the story involves a pirate, the teacher could bring in a toy parrot or wear an eye patch. If the story involves an animal, the teacher could display a similar stuffed animal in the classroom

New Book Advertisements

Design a billboard bulletin board that advertises new books. The children can make posters of their favorite books—books that they think other children would enjoy reading.

Book Exchange

Ask several other classes to join the fun! Prepare a presentation of some of your favorite stories. Each classroom takes a turn and presents their books. Then the classes can exchange the books. A later discussion between the classes about the books can be fun too!

Sound Effects

Sound effects can add excitement to almost any story. Tape recordings can be made of rain, wind, and other weather conditions; the children can record cheering, booing, and laughing; and stories with repeated phrases can be recorded, such as "I'll huff and I'll puff and I'll blow your house down." Children will enjoy anticipating hearing the sound effects.

New Ideas and Concepts That Could Be Helpful for Some People with Dyslexia

Font Information for Dyslexic Readers

Some individuals with dyslexia believe the length of the ascenders and descenders of letters in a word affects their ability to visually recall the shape of the word. If ascenders and descenders are too short, the shape of the word is more difficult to identify. Although this has not been proven by scientific research, it has been noted by many individuals that clear sans-serif fonts are easier to read.

Fonts that have received positive feedback for being easier to read (shown in 14 point type):

❑ **Arial:** Aa Bb Cc Dd Ee Ff Gg Hh Ii Jj Kk Ll Mm Nn Oo Pp Qq Rr Ss Tt Uu Vv Ww Xx Yy Zz

❑ **Geneva:** Aa Bb Cc Dd Ee Ff Gg Hh Ii Jj Kk Ll Mm Nn Oo Pp Qq Rr Ss Tt Uu Vv Ww Xx Yy Zz

❑ **Trebuchet MS:** Aa Bb Cc Dd Ee Ff Gg Hh Ii Jj Kk Ll Mm Nn Oo Pp Qq Rr Ss Tt Uu Vv Ww Xx Yy Zz

❑ **Sassoon:** Aa Bb Cc Dd Ee Ff Gg Hh Ii Jj Kk Ll Mm Nn Oo Pp Qq Rr Ss Tt Uu Vv Ww Xx Yy Zz

❑ **Comic Sans:** Aa Bb Cc Dd Ee Ff Gg Hh Ii Jj Kk Ll Mm Nn Oo Pp Qq Rr Ss Tt Uu Vv Ww Xx Yy Zz

❑ **Myriad Pro:** Aa Bb Cc Dd Ee Ff Gg Hh Ii Jj Kk Ll Mm Nn Oo Pp Qq Rr Ss Tt Uu Vv Ww Xx Yy Zz

(Myriad Pro in 10 point type has been used for the main body of text in this book.)

What Are Colored Overlays? Are They Helpful?

Many people with dyslexia have claimed that their reading skills greatly improved after they began wearing eyeglasses with colored lenses or when they placed colored transparencies over the print they were reading. It is imperative to state that although many people have experienced improved reading using colored lenses or overlays—these colored materials DO NOT CURE dylexia—and that this color treatment is not even appropriate for everyone who has dyslexia.

Here is why using colored lenses or colored overlays **may** or **may not** be beneficial for a student with dyslexia: It is estimated that 15 percent of the general population and as many as 46 percent of struggling readers may also have a condition known as **scotopic sensitivity syndrome (SSS)** or **Irlen syndrome**. This syndrome is named after the psychologist Helen Irlen, who discovered over 25 years ago that some individuals showed a marked improvement in their reading skills when print was covered by colored acetate sheets. This condition is not an optical problem, but rather a problem with how the brain processes visual information.

Some of the difficulties that people with SSS/Irlen syndrome experience are:

- ❏ letter or word reversals
- ❏ eye strain, headaches, or watery eyes
- ❏ slow, choppy reading
- ❏ poor comprehension
- ❏ print looks "different"; it appears blurry, moves, or disappears
- ❏ being bothered by bright or fluorescent lights
- ❏ misreading of words

- ❏ problems tracking text
- ❏ skipping words or whole lines
- ❏ appearing tired, dizzy, or moody
- ❏ disliking to read
- ❏ trouble copying letters or words
- ❏ inconsistent letter size
- ❏ inconsistent letter and word spacing
- ❏ poor spelling

The difficulties above look very similar to the difficulties associated with dyslexia. The difference is that for people who simply have SSS/Irlen syndrome, the use of colored lenses or colored overlays can actually stop the print from blurring and moving—thus allowing the individual to see print that is "clear" and "still" and finally be given the opportunity to learn to read.

However, because numerous research studies have suggested that 46 percent of struggling readers may also have SSS/Irlen syndrome, it is always advisable to have children's vision examined by an ophthalmologist or development optometrist. If you notice a student complaining of bright lights, headaches, or watery eyes or if the student expresses that print seem blurry, moves, or vanishes, it may be valuable to have the child assessed at an Irlen Center. The child would first be evaluated to discover if color overlays do in fact seem to help the child's visual perception of print. If color is found to be helpful, then further diagnostic work needs to be completed to determine the most effective color for that child. (For more information go to: www.irlen.com.)

In the meantime, you may purchase color overlays at most any art store or use any of the color transparencies included in the back of this book to see if a child expresses any benefit when using a color transparency when reading. *(Cut carefully along the dashed lines and use only one color at a time.)*

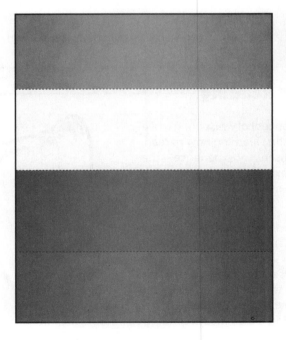

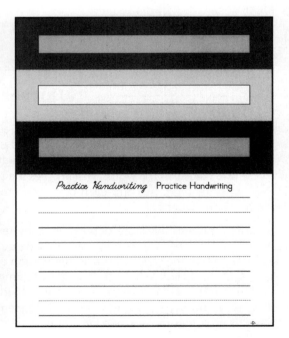

The Value of Reading Aloud

Everyone knows there is tremendous value in reading aloud to children. To name just a few of the benefits, reading aloud can motivate learning, strengthen reading skills, help develop phonological awareness, and enhance vocabulary. These are not new ideas or concepts, but they are important enough to be mentioned in this section.

Recent reading research from the National Institute of Child Health and Development (NICHD) and the National Reading Panel (NRP) have identified some strategies that may not be new to teachers, but they have now been documented and proven as effective. One of those strategies is called *monitored oral reading*—a challenging task for a child with dyslexia, but also a strategy that can improve fluency. In monitored oral reading, a student will read aloud at an independent level while a teacher, parent, or peer monitors any errors.

The following has been suggested by NICHD to determine a student's independent reading level:

❏ To read at an **independent level**, children read with ease and find no more than 1 in 20 words difficult to read (95 percent success).

❏ To read at an **instructional level**, children will find the text challenging but will struggle to read no more than 1 in 10 words (90 percent success).

❏ To read at a **frustration level**, children will find the text difficult and will struggle reading more than 1 in 10 words (less than 90 percent success).

The following are some successful monitored oral reading strategies:

❏ **Student reading aloud with an adult.** The adult reads the text first while the student listens. Then, the student reads and rereads the text until fluency is achieved.

❏ **Choral readings.** A group of students read the same text together in unison.

❏ **Reading along with taped-recorded text.** The student reads along, tracking the text as he listens to the recorded fluent reader. Books on tape can be used, or a teacher or parent can make tape recordings for the student.

❏ **Peer reading.** Students are partners and take turns reading aloud to one another. Generally, the partner who reads first is the more fluent reader.

"Whisper" Reading

Another facet of the strategy of reading aloud is the new concept of whispering while reading. Most of us have observed that when a young child is first learning how to read, she will often mouth or whisper the words. This creates a multisensory experience—the child touches the book or tracks the words, visually sees the text, and then hears herself as she whispers while reading. This approach does seem to make sense in practicing reading with struggling readers.

There are several "phones" available for purchase commercially (see illustration) that children may hold and whisper into as they read. A child's quiet whispering is amplified through the phone so that the child hears a louder version of what she is reading. One company claims that a child is able to hear phonemes 10 times more clearly when using the company's phone. The author was not able to find hard evidence to support this, but the multisensory approach does make educational sense, and—it looks like fun! Anything that adds enjoyment to a struggling student's reading experience is certainly worth looking into.
